I dedicate my first book in my second language to

- ○ God, who created me and my passion to write.

- ○ Mohamed Aly, my husband who supported me, and helped me from A to Z.

- ○ Moez and Marwan, my amazing sons and their future as American Muslims.

- ○ all peaceful American Muslims who might suffer or worry as a misunderstood minority.

Contents

Foreword
by Glen Heefner

Your father has traveled 20 hours, nearly halfway around the world. He is fascinated by nearly everything he sees. Still, he has made this journey really to see you and your family—not to see this land whose language he taught to you even though he himself has never been here. You take him to a place you know he will love, a place where each and all of you together will be delighted to spend the beautiful day. You thought of everything, everything but the shock of being unwelcome there.

But the story does not end with this shock. The chapters titled "Unforgettable Moments," taken together, tell the whole story; a story of people, not places. The entire collection in this book has this thread: the more people learn, the more they tend to allow their best selves to guide their behavior. Bad actors in these stories don't get comcuppance. They get a window, a view to see part of their world through fresh eyes. They get an opportunity to become their own best.

Much of this book is an expansive examination of cultural and religious traditions. Its chapters titled "Cultural Differences," "Interesting Information," and "True or False" provide historical and ethnic context. This allows readers to gently fall backward into a cradle of new understanding. It shows them that, without dissimilar people in the world, traditions are simply revered practices; that only the presence of some who are captive to their own apprehensions has gotten us calling these things *differences*.

There is plenty here on matters of faith and how these often direct one's hand. Those chapters dig to the roots of Islam and provide examples, some hypothetical but never far-flung, all deeply personal. It's sad that, in order to see another person's faith, we have to borrow their eyes; but such *is* faith, right? A trust in things unseen.

Zeithar explores the liberties and rights that underpin social interactions in Western societies. I can still hear the rhyme, "Sticks and stones may break my bones but words will never hurt me," the salve my parents so hopefully applied to abrasions that thoughtless remarks of other kids had etched into my heart. Does our embraceable freedom of speech have any attached responsibility? Do words that effervesce from our printers and our tongues ever leave an ugly precipitate that's too crusty to scrub? This topic in her book has sent me out to survey damage. She discusses the rights of women and what is uniquely expected of them. And also the dark cloud of politics and dominion hovering above the countless unlikely friendships that sprout and flourish anyway, joyfully defiant, in the shadow of that cloud.

This book isn't about intolerance; it's about hurtfulness. Alternately, it isn't about tolerance; it's about appreciation. Sitting across a conference table from Rania Zeithar, as I have many times, has always had me hunker to wait, like a kid at Christmas, for the gift I knew was coming: the gift of broader eyesight. As you read this account of her experiences in Saudi Arabia, Egypt, and the USA, you'll have my seat at that table. Being there may make you want to discard some preconceptions and start over as an observer of life at its essence, where it is lived, whether half a world away or in your own backyard. Enjoy the privilege.

Glen Heefner is a technical writer and an author of literary short fiction. He lives in the mountains of north Georgia.

Foreword
by Rev. David E. Dean

Our world needs more civil discourse. In this volume, instead of caustic language, broad generalizations, abusive and derogatory accusations, and authoritarian adversarial broadsides, Rania provides reasoned, personal, and enlightened observations of life in America during the volatile years since 9/11.

Like most Americans I felt the shock, bewilderment, and the onset of terror when the Muslim extremists attacked the Twin Towers. Much of my perception of Muslims and Islam was formulated in the ensuing news coverage and heightened awareness of the role of Islam in our world. Unlike many in my country I believed I already possessed a foundational knowledge of Islam. Had I not studied world religions in college and seminary? I unquestioningly believed I grasped the complexities of Islamic terrorism and my country's appropriate response.

Then I met Rania Zeithar, a Muslim American woman from Egypt. She joined the writers group I attend because she wanted feedback on her blogs, since English is her second language. In getting the group's feedback, Rania shattered my preconceived ideas regarding Muslim women in particular. I wondered what the impact would be on my view of Muslims in general. Soon I realized how insightfully she observed American culture and found many of her insights encouraging and refreshing.

Take the Hijab, for example. Before Rania shared her blog on the Hijab, I felt an uneasy sympathy with a common impression found on social media. The Hijab represented repression of women and somehow didn't fit American culture. I say I had an uneasy sympathy. That hesitation came from my understanding of my own Christian faith.

Did not my scriptures in 1 Corinthians 11:6 instruct women to keep their heads covered? Yet, the same people who condemn the Hijab are the ones who dismiss the Biblical injunction as culturally irrelevant. They do this without considering the possibility of other people finding a head covering culturally relevant.

I also know that within the broad Protestant Christian faith tradition, there are groups—including some Mennonites and the Amish—among whom the women cover their heads with special bonnets. Although not exactly like the Hijab, they serve a similar function. Yet I have never heard anyone state the Amish bonnet should be banned in courtrooms. And in the Christian faith traditions, which have religious orders, frequently nuns wear head coverings. In many cases the religious habit covers more than the Hijab but not quite as much as the common portrayal of the burka, which only has an opening for they eyes. Yet, despite the similarities, I have not heard calls to ban nuns from wearing habits.

Rania's blog about the Hijab produced a profound reorientation of my views on Islamic culture. I felt so deeply about this I responded in my blog, which Rania has graciously included in this volume.

Without getting to know Rania as a person, I would have missed out on the pleasure of genuine civil discourse. As if accompanying her on her adventure in America, I felt sadness at discrimination, joy at self-discovery, and love of family and faith. Had I not been willing to listen (which is an admonition of my own faith in James 1:19) I would have missed this opportunity as well as a fresh glimpse into my own culture.

Like many Americans I discounted the opinions of people from other cultural backgrounds. I believed they hated America and Americans. Perhaps I had seen too many news clips of crowds holding placards stating "Down with America." Yet, through the civil discourse Rania offered, I came to understand that some of "them" actually appreciate American culture and see our cultural glass as half full.

I suspect a partial reason why Americans downplay the opinions of other countries is because we inwardly believe we are deficient. We filter our view of ourselves through the lens of what we believe we should be and we find ourselves lacking. For example, consider the raging debates about our current health care situation. The discourse around this topic is anything but civil. In our passion to improve we disparage what we have, as well as those who disagree with us. Or consider the handicapped in our country. Can't we do more for them than simply reserve parking places? Shouldn't we do more for those will mental illnesses? The debate rages on. Discourse often less than civil. Or consider diversity. We view our country as fragmented into isolated groups. Discussion around the diversity within our country frequently focuses on who has what, who has deprived whom of what, and how to rectify the injustice. The lack of civil discourse has degenerated into violence far too frequently.

Most of us want to improve these situations, yet we remain divided. When we promote our positions as the only ones, we stifle civil discourse. By viewing our cultural cup as half empty we strive harder to get others to agree with us. How engaging to find Rania presenting, in these pages, a different perspective. She sees America's cultural cup as half full. Without hearing her, I would have missed considering American life and culture from a fresh perspective. To see my world with new eyes is a precious gift of civil discourse.

When I spoke of my pleasure over Rania's civil discourse, some of my acquaintances expressed concern. "Don't you realize," (I paraphrase) "that it's all a part of an Islamic plot to destroy our way of life? ISIS claims to represent Islam. They engage in extreme acts of terrorism. Therefore all Muslims are willing to do anything to destroy Western culture." This way of thinking clearly represents the lack of civil discourse. The logic is also deeply flawed. If I changed the name of the group, here's the logic: "The Ku Klux Klan claims to be Christian. They engage in extreme acts of racial discrimination. Therefore all Christians practice radical racial discrimination."

As a Christian, I find this logic offensive because the faith I practice and the Bible I read does not promote the extreme behavior of the KKK. That is exactly why groups like ISIS and the KKK are called extremist groups. They do not represent the mainstream. Isn't it about time to stop labeling one another and instead listen to each other?

The heart of civil discourse is listening to what people say for, and about, themselves. Uncivil discourse tells other people what they believe. Let's redirect American discourse back to the heart of civility: "Do to others as you would have them do to you."

Civil discourse does not mean agreement. Rania and I disagree on some major points, among which are: who the Lord Jesus Christ is and who the Prophet Mohammed is. This does not mean that I cannot listen to, respect, and interact with Rania with civility and so receive the gift of her insights and perspectives.

So, if you are ready for a journey into civil discourse, if you are ready to hear Rania speak for herself, if you are ready to have your preconceptions challenged, if you are open to broadening your understanding and knowledge, then continue reading. Civil discourse—let the adventure begin.

Reverend Dean writes both science fiction and Christian prose and pastors the Advent Christian Church in DeKalb, Illinois. He is the author of There is a Dragon in My Bedroom, *contributed to* Infinite Monkeys: Tales of Redemption, *and with his wife co-authored with him* Philippine Reflections. *He also maintains a blog at* https://davedeanblog.wordpress.com.

Introduction

For me *America Through My Eyes* is not just words, pages, ideas, feelings and thoughts; it is a hope I once thought was impossible, because I couldn't understand the English language. This book is a way to open my heart and my mind to the world, so the readers see who I am, how I think, what I feel and what I believe. It's my humble attempt to counteract what politics and the media are doing in our world. This book represents the love that I send from my heart to every soul on earth.

Right before the time to publish my book, I got these words as a nice surprise:

> *Reading was not a subject I was fond of when I was a child; math was by far my favorite. All that changed a few years ago when I began reading Rania's writings.*
>
> *At first, I just read them to be supportive, to make her happy, and to avoid getting into trouble. After I read her third story (In Arabic), I began to love reading, always looking forward to her next story. Although I was a part of some of the stories, reading about the events from her perspective gave me a more complete picture and enabled me to truly feel her emotions. Rania's writing allows the readers to feel a part of the stories as if they were their own.*

I will do my best to be supportive so that Rania is able to continue to do her best writing.

Rania, you are the best story that has happened to me and I am so glad to be a part of your life."

Your husband,
Mohamed Aly

America Through My Eyes

1   My Hijab

I'll write about the most common question I've heard here in the U.S. Sometimes I hear people's words directly from their questions or even silently from their eyes when they see me with my Hijab; meaning I cover my hair and body. "Why?" "Why are you covering your beauty?" How can you handle your scarves in the summer and all these clothes over your body? Don't you feel hot?" Or I notice some people looking at me as a *poor* Muslim lady: "Somebody forced her to wear that thing." I actually heard that from a  kind old lady a couple of years ago. Some other people will look at me in the open park or on the beach on a hot summer day, with all my clothes and scarf on as a totally crazy women. I can see this meaning clearly in their eyes.

The truth is that I'm not the person they see in their eyes. For any woman, her beauty is an important thing. Any lady likes to see herself beautiful and feels happy when the others notice it!

My Hijab

But, the point most people don't know is that my Hijab was all my decision. I began to wear Hijab when I was 23 years old. My dad, my husband or my brothers never asked me once to wear it. I started to wear it in the U.S., not in Egypt. Before I decided to wear my Hijab, I was married. And I used to wear shorts, short skirts, short-sleeve shirts and dresses, all kinds of clothes you see in the stores, just like any young lady in my age.

The question now you ask is why? Why did I leave all these fun things and decided to change my life with my Hijab? Is it because I'm a Muslim lady, and all Muslim ladies have to do it? No, because not all of Muslim ladies wear Hijab. Some of my friends and family are Muslims and don't wear Hijab. They are very good people. I think some of them are even better Muslims than I am! Then, what is the point? Let me give you an example to explain my idea.

In any relationship in our lives, we usually go through different levels of feelings. First, you know someone then, you feel him in your life. Then, you like him. After that, you believe him. Finally, you love and trust him. I went through all these feelings with people in my life. I'm sure you did with someone in your life also. However, my husband is a normal person. He doesn't have any super powers. He is a human just like me and you, but I still trust him because I know what his strengths and weaknesses are. He is amazing with road directions. If I go with him anywhere, I'll never think about the way, because I trust him in navigating more than I trust myself. I myself usually get lost on my way to any new place, and sometime to old places too! I trust that he will take me safely to the right place.

My Hijab

Now let's use the same philosophy about God, who created me. I was nothing. He made me. He knows me more than I know myself. I felt my God. I knew my God. I believed him, I loved him, I trusted him, and I felt all his strengths. Through these steps, I learned more about my religion. I understood the reasons for how and why I worship God, by reading the Quran, the prophet's words and some good books. I didn't stop with that, I even used the opportunity of being in the U.S. and started to read about all of the other religions I've heard about.

That was so useful for me as a Muslim lady who was born in a Muslim family inside an Islamic country. In Egypt, 90% of the population is Muslim and 10% is Orthodox Christians. I didn't have the chance in Egypt to know or learn about any other religions, but I got this great chance in the U.S. That's why I feel so sad when I see a young girl, just a child, wearing Hijab even though God didn't ask her to do this before being an adult. Also she missed going through all these wonderful steps toward her God and missed being able to make her decision all by herself when she feels like she wants to do it and is ready to do it.

Wearing Hijab in my religion is not about wearing a piece of cloth on my head or covering my body from the public eyes. It is much more, it's a way of life. I have to be responsible about all my actions and words when I talk or deal with people anywhere. With my Hijab, I'm not being just myself but I'm also being my religion, and sometimes I am all the people who follow this religion in the world. Especially in a country like the U.S.

Most of the American people have no idea about Islam, except from the unfair media. So when they see a lady who lies to get something that doesn't belong to her, when she is wearing Hijab,

My Hijab

I'll never blame them when they say in their mind or their words "That women did so because she is a Muslim." It's not their fault or the media's fault. It's all her fault. She thought that covering her outside will save her from any other sin from the inside and that is not right. She got it backwards and she also forgot that her look will not make them think she is a bad person but they will think she is from a bad religion, especially with the media effect.

Wearing my Hijab in the U.S. is a kind of challenge for me, just because mostly I deal with people who look at me as a different kind of person, not really me, as I mentioned before; or people who hate me right away because they knew from the first second I'm a Muslim; or people will look at my poor, kind, nice husband as an evil eastern Muslim man! But on the inside I live in peace.

If I'm sure that God loves me, then I know he will never ask me for something that will make me suffer. Even if I cover some of my beauty by wearing my Hijab, I got the spiritual strength in my soul, and I do feel much happier in my life. With my Hijab, I know I won't be judged by how short my skirt is, how well I have my hair done, or how perfect my body shape is. But my personality, my soul and my behavior will appear the most.

When I was 10 years old, I asked my mom, "Why did you begin to wear Hijab when you were 35 years old?" She replied "I'll never take it off, even for a million pounds [the Egyptian currency]!" I didn't understand the meaning of her answer then. I heard that a long time ago and, back then, I would never think that I would share my mom's words one day from my heart, but I do now.

I worship my God every time I wear my Hijab and go out in public. I'm telling him, "I love you, God, more than anything else in my life." I swear if someone will offer me a billion dollars or more to take off my Hijab, I'll never think about it. This feeling is really worth for me more than money.

Here are some answers for the most common questions I was asked during my life with Hijab in the USA:

- I stay home without my Hijab.
- I don't sleep with my Hijab.
- I don't take shower with my Hijab on.
- I get a haircut, hair styles, hair dying and highlights.
- Around my family and my girlfriends, I take my Hijab off and wear nice clothes that don't have to cover my entire body.
- Sometimes my Hijab makes me feel hot in the summer, but it is always a blessing in the winter.

I hope you can understand now why I decided to wear my Hijab and how I wear it.

With all my respect!!!

2   Us and Them—Me and You
by David Dean
(a response to Chapter 1, My Hijab)

I attend my writers group to encourage other writers and to develop my skills. My intention is not to have my worldview challenged. But that is precisely what occurred recently. I confronted how neatly I compartmentalize my world, something I don't particularly like.

I divide my world into Us and Them. I separate the people in my world into groups based on any number of criteria: politics (Republicans and Democrats), ideologies (Liberal and Conservative), economics (rich and poor), religion (Catholic and Protestant) and, recently, culturally (Muslim extremists and Western Culture). That which disconcerts me most about this tendency is that, by dividing my world into Us and Them, I convince myself We are right and They are wrong. We are good and They are bad. The worst part about this tendency is that it allows me to dehumanize Them and lump all of Them into one category.

Thus, dismissing them, I am free to continue as I am, comfortable in my superiority. I not only can avoid seeing myself and possible inconsistencies in my outlook, but also don't have to engage Them because They aren't worth the effort. Perhaps the most obvious example is the tragic world situation involving Muslim extremists. Because this group of Muslims commits egregious acts in the name if Islam, I have found it easy to lump all Muslims together as unworthy of consideration.

That was my perception until a few months ago, when I moderated my local writers group meeting. In came Rania, a vivacious, enchanting, articulate Egyptian Muslin woman. She attended to improve her English writing.

I knew she was Muslim from her Hijab head scarf. Instead of distancing myself from her I felt empathy. I, too, lived in a "foreign" country for four years. I struggled to communicate in a different language. I know how much effort (and courage) it takes to immerse myself in another culture. Yet, Rania seems almost effortless in her interactions in our group. I admire how clearly Rania expresses herself not just verbally, but also in writing. As a member of the writers group, I willingly offer suggestions from my intuitive knowledge of English, but that is merely to tweak her communication.

That is not all. I have received from her as much as, if not more than, what I've given. As Rania has shared her observations of my North American culture, I have seen with new appreciation some of the positive aspects of my culture, even as I re-examine some ways I'm used to doing things.

She also shared her background and her life as a Muslim in America. At the writers group, Rania recently shared reactions to her Hijab. Surprisingly, I found common ground with her as she shared her rationale for wearing this traditional head scarf. I'll let her speak for herself:

> In any relationship in our lives, we usually go through
> different levels of feelings. First, you know someone then,
> you feel him in your life. Then, you like him. After that,

you believe him. Finally, you love and trust him. I went through all these feelings with people in my life. I'm sure you did with someone in your life also. However, my husband is a normal person. He doesn't have any super powers. He is a human just like me and you, but I still trust him because I know what his strengths and weaknesses are. He is amazing with road directions. If I go with him anywhere, I'll never think about the way, because I trust him in navigating more than I trust myself. I myself usually get lost on my way to any new place, and sometime to old places too! I trust that he will take me safely to the right place.

Now let's use the same philosophy about God, who created me. I was nothing. He made me. He knows me more than I know myself. I felt my God. I knew my God. I believed him, I loved him, I trusted him, and I felt all his strengths. Through these steps, I learned more about my religion. I understood the reasons for how and why I worship God, by reading the Quran, the prophet's words and some good books.

Until reading this, I never considered the possibility a Muslim could grow in their understanding of and trust in their God. This desire to love God more deeply and follow Him more fully is the heart of my spiritual journey. I long to develop this attitude and I desire to help others develop deeper trust in God. Because Rania joined the writers group, I can no longer combine all Muslims into the collective Them. Rania is a You.

My interaction with Rania shattered my monolithic perception of Muslims. I deeply appreciate her vulnerability and insights. I may not affirm the tenets of Islam; nor do I know how many other

Muslims are like Rania, but I cannot deny her kindred heart beating as mine.

For that I am grateful.

3   The Turning Point

I will never forget that sound at my grandma's house: very loud screaming, crying and knocking so hard on the wall. The wall was between me and that person. I was a little child then. When I heard these weird sounds, I ran so fast to my mom with all kinds of fear, asking, "Mom, what is this weird sound I'm hearing? Something wrong is happening in our neighbors' apartment."

My mom answered kindly, "No, dear, don't worry! Our neighbor Anga...she has a brother, and he is so sick. He makes these sounds once a while, even since I was a child."

I asked her with wonder, "Is he an old man, Mom?"

"Yes!" she said.

I asked again, "Why don't they take him to the doctor, so he can help him?"

"Nobody can help him, Rania. He will be like this forever," she said.

I spent a lot of my early childhood in my grandma's house, and I'll never forget that person and that day when I saw his old face and his gray hair for a few seconds, when his scary old sister opened their door to get in the house, and I was going out with my grandma at the same time.

"Why does he never leave the house?" I asked my grandma.

"He can't. He's not a normal person, Rania, and he's crazy. His sister keeps him in the house all the time, so he will not get hurt or run away, and so nobody will make fun of him..."

In Egypt and in almost all of the poor counties, having a special need child is a disaster for the whole family. WHY?

Because, in a poor country, they try hard to educate the regular students for free, so there are no chances for a special needs kid to be in a public school. If the parents are rich, which is rare, he will be in a private school just for special needs. If not, which is the usual case, he will live his life in his room forever. So the generations never get the chance to know these kids, talk with them, help them or even love them. The only feeling they ever get for them, if they see them in the streets, is to be scared of them.

THIS IS MY BACKGROUND!

When I started to find a job and I was told about working in the Special Education field, I was shocked for a second. I couldn't imagine that happening. I was sure I wouldn't be able to do it. I told myself, *If these kids have mental disabilities, I'll be scared. If they have physical disabilities, I'll be full of pity for them.* How hard that would be for me!

But I decided to try and, if I can't handle it, I'll easily quit.

I started my mystery job, and what happened was something I was not expecting at all. Since my first day, I have learned amazing things about these kids and, through the years, day after day, I've seen what I call miracles compared to my early childhood experiences. It's so hard to explain my feelings when I see these kids are improving every day, and I've seen them getting closer and closer to being a "regular" person. I'm a little part of a huge system that helps them become an effective part in our life and to depend on themselves in life much more than anyone else. I really have learned a lot from them and about them. I can say loudly, THEY CHANGED SO MANY THINGS INSIDE ME. They gave me the chance to see a new wonderful world: full of beauty, innocence and love.

Working in Special Ed is one of the best things that has happened to me.

Sometimes I remember my feelings toward my poor neighbor when I was 6 years old and compare it to my feelings toward my students now. It amazes me how life can change us from one side to the opposite.

I really wish to live until I see the day when Egypt will be able to educate and care about the special kids just as much as those who are not disabled.

4   English and Me

A blank piece of paper and a pen will make me full of happiness and pleasure. Reading and writing are two of my favorite things to do in life. When I try to remember how and when I started to love and enjoy them, so many pictures come to my mind. I see Egypt, my homeland. I see Alexandria, my beloved city. I see the amazing shore of the Mediterranean Sea. I feel the fresh sea breeze. I watch the waves chasing each other and sending me little drops of water before they disappear. I see the sun spreading all my favorite colors on the clear blue sky before it goes behind the sea to make my favorite view, the sunset. Alexandria is not a desert and it has no camels; it's just an attractive old city, full of beautiful buildings, cars, and kind people. I also see my family's first old house. I see shelves full of books, my room, my study desk, and my dad.

My dad was a perfect model for a learner. He suffered a lot in his life to learn and to earn his degree. He is the one who made me love to read and made me a lover of the English language. He used to sit with me for hours studying English, and teach me some tricks to help me remember the hard English words or the translation in Arabic. Maybe that's why I usually had my highest grades in Arabic, English, and French. My dad used to give me so many books from his own old ones, the ones he had since he was young. I read all kind of books, Arabic literature and translated English literature too, like Agatha Christie and Ernest Hemingway books. I started to write poems when I was nine years old. By then I had my first Arabic poetry notebook.

English was my second language to learn at school from kindergarten to college. In Egypt we learn the British English at schools, but we never have the chance or the ability to use it, so I was good with writing but bad with speaking and listening. That was my challenge with English when I came to the USA. I couldn't understand the American accent at all. It was so hard for me to interact with my community or even enjoy my life. Everything was in English, all the TV channels, the radio, the neighbors, even the books and the magazines. At that time I had no computer either. I used to stay alone at my apartment for a long day, from 7:00 a.m. to 8:30 p.m., with nothing but some Arabic books I brought with me from Egypt, my pen and my notebook.

One of the easiest questions anyone may have in an English test when I was at school in Egypt was about dialogue, and the easiest part in any dialogue is the end, when *Person A* says, "Thank you," and *Person B* replies, "Not at all." That was the reply we had been taught from our English teachers all years at schools. When I came to the U.S., the first time I went out. I went shopping at Wal-Mart with my husband. I held the door for a lady, who was behind me. She smiled and said, "Thank you." I smiled back and replied with all the self-confidence I had, "Not at all." I will never forget the look that lady gave to me on that day. She looked at me as an alien who had just come from Mars. My husband looked at me and said, "Rania! I forgot to tell you. They don't use these words here to in reply to a thank-you. They use *You're welcome* instead."

I was so nervous to talk with anyone in English, or even try to make friends. After my very social life in Egypt, which was full of family and friends, I had nobody to talk with in the USA but my husband. He never lost hope in me. He kept asking me to go out, pushing me to talk with people and encouraging me to break from my fears and try.

Finally, I listened to him and did it! The first time I made the decision to go out, I went to meet some ladies from the neighborhood. It was a Bingo game, which took place in the clubhouse every Wednesday morning. I was so nervous and worried. Will they accept me? Can they understand my bad English with my bad accent? What would be their reaction if they talked to me and I couldn't understand them? All kinds of these questions I had in my head on that morning.

I remember that day very well. It was 10:00 a.m., in the winter. It was so cold, the snow was covering everything in the streets. I arrived at the clubhouse and entered. It smelled like a pine tree. The room was decorated very well for the event. In the far corner of the room was a small table full of little gifts. I figured out later, it was for the game winners. I saw a group of seven ladies sitting around a table in the side of the room.

They looked at me. I smiled and said, "Hi," then I sat down on one of the chairs by the table. One of the ladies looked at me and asked me a question. I couldn't understand a word from her question. I felt so bad and even more nervous. I told her, "I'm so sorry, my English is so bad. Can you say it again slowly please?" She smiled and said, "Yes! Sure I can!" And her smile remained.

She asked me, "Where are you from? And how long have you been in the USA?" I answered her questions and they all welcomed me. We started to play after they taught me how to play the new game (Bingo). That was my first time ever to play it. I had beginner's luck that day. I won Bingo three times that morning. I had so much fun. They all were so nice and they even asked me to join them every Wednesday morning. Since then, Wednesdays started to be my most important and fun days for a long time, just to play Bingo and to see my new friends.

After I moved from that complex, I kept in touch with most of those ladies for a long time, but eventually I lost contact with them. I owe this group of ladies a lot, not just because they helped me to improve my English with their patience and support, but I owe them everything good that happened in my life after I met them: my job, my good American friends, and even being here at this moment. Sometimes, I just imagine if they hadn't accepted me, welcomed me, shown me their beautiful smiles the first time I met them, helped me and supported me. For sure I wouldn't be myself now! These ladies gave me one of the most important lessons of my life—*Just one smile may change a person's life.*

5 Cultural Differences in Daily Life

It is very interesting, exciting and sometimes embarrassing to live between two different cultures. There are many cultural differences I notice between Egypt and the U.S., and I will do my best to pick the most interesting things for you here.

Food at Gatherings

In my Arabic culture, food is a big deal. If I invite someone in Egypt, a family member or a friend to my house, I have to cook a lot of food. Not two or three but five or more different kinds of food. In my culture that shows how much you love the person you are inviting, how happy you are to have them, and it demonstrates your generosity. On the other hand, as a guest, you have to eat all the food that you get on your plate every couple minutes, or until you feel you really will explode. If you don't eat, it means you don't like the food or you are not happy to be there. You should try your best to ignore how full you are, or how the food tastes. Now you can tell how much I love, enjoy and appreciate the American culture in a gathering. Having friends over in the U.S never stresses me out or makes me tired. If I cook any dish for them, or have one dish at their house, it is just perfect. In Egypt, it is also very rude to ask a visitor to bring food with him to your house. And it is rude if you ask to take food home with you when you leave the hosts. These last two things are very common in U.S, and I agree 100% with the American culture on that point.

The Bidets

Maybe it sounds weird for you, but believe me, this is a huge cultural difference between the U.S and Egypt or any Middle Eastern country. In all of Egypt, for example, there are no bathrooms without a bidet—in houses, stores, or even along the streets. As an Egyptian, I can tell you that the people in Egypt usually look at the U.S as a better place. We believe it is much more advanced in the use of hygienic supplies, and technology as well. It is completely shocking for any Arabic foreigner, the first time they use the bathroom in the airport. I remember my very first day in the U.S, when I spent around 15 minutes in the airport's bathroom trying to search in every single spot for a bidet. I was very sure it is somewhere in there, but it was all my problem—that I couldn't find it because it is very technological. I will never forget how surprised I was when I found out that American people don't use a bidet. It is the same surprise I see on my Americans friends' faces when they see I have a bidet at my house. A bathroom without a bidet in my culture is like a bathroom without a faucet in the American culture.

Welcome and Goodbye

When you welcome a person or say goodbye to him, you usually shake hands. Sometimes you may hug or kiss. That works in two different ways between USA and Egypt. In the U.S., if you meet a new person, you just shake hands. If the person is a close friend, male or female, you usually hug that person or kiss from one side with the hug. In Egypt, the majority of the people just shake hands when they meet a new person. About close friends, if both are females, they hug with one kiss on each cheek. If both friends are males, they hug with three or four kisses. If the friends are a male and a female, they just shake hands with no hugs or kisses. You may wonder why, or might ask what these people think of their friends? I have friends who are male and female. My husband and my brother also have friends who are male and female. All of our friends, in our thoughts are just friends, but any kind of touching in my culture and religion is limited. That is a cultural thing, not just for Muslims. Even the Egyptians who are Christians follow the same custom. So when we are in the States and I get a hug from a male, or my husband gets a hug from a female, we feel as you might if you go to Egypt and get four kisses on your cheeks from a new friend—weird. Any culture varies within any society, and in Egypt too, about 10% of the people will not follow this custom and they usually act more like the Western culture. On the other hand, about 10% will not even touch anyone not related to them from a different gender, and if they have to, they wear gloves. I respect everyone's choice, but I feel more comfortable to be one of the 80%.

If I had the power to change cultures, I would give the American food gatherings to Egypt, would bring bidets to the U.S., and would leave welcomes and goodbyes as they are.

Daily Life

6 Cultural Differences in Major Life Events

In this chapter of cultural differences, I'll talk about major life events; things such as birth, birthdays, marriage, and death. These life events usually are so different from one culture to another. I'll do my best to give you a full, clear, image about these differences between Egypt and the U.S.

Birth

In the U.S., when a woman is pregnant, she usually lives a normal life. She works and does her chores normally; she just is more careful about what she eats and drinks. One of her friends or her family members holds a baby shower for her, which is a nice party. During that party, she gets almost everything she needs for the new baby from her friends and family. This party is usually a couple of months before her due date. After she has had her baby, she quickly goes back to her normal life.

In Egypt, when a lady knows she is pregnant, she will not do anything she used to do. She'll reduce all her efforts by 30% to 70% in work or chores. If she just thinks about doing regular things like walking, sports, or deep house cleaning, her husband and family will intervene right away and will deal with her like she is trying to kill herself and her baby. In Egypt, they celebrate the baby after he or she comes, most of the time a week or two after the birth. The family holds a big party for all the family and the friends. If the family can, they make a big dinner for everyone with lots of meat (which we call *Aqeqa*). If they can't afford this, they serve packets of candy, nuts, chocolate and a small souvenir with the baby's name and birth date. All the children hold candles and go around the baby, everyone sings silly and funny songs for the baby. Also in Egypt, the parents dress the baby in so many layers either in summer or winter. They don't take him outside the house the first month of his life, except if there's an emergency. They think that, if the baby goes out or has fewer layers of clothes, the baby will get sick right away.

Birthdays

There are not that many differences between birthday parties in Egypt and in the U.S. Cake, candles, wishes, gifts, and the Arabic version of the happy birthday song: *Happy year for you beautiful, happy year for you beautiful, happy year for you* [name]*, happy year for you beautiful*. The only big difference I can see is in opening the gifts. In the U.S., the birthday person opens, during the party, all the gifts they get, and in the front of everyone. In Egypt this is an inappropriate thing to do. There are two reasons: first, if I show much excitement for the gift, it might mean that I invited you for the gift, or that the gift is more important to me than the guest himself; second, maybe one guest brings a smaller gift and another brings a big expensive one, so opening both in front of everyone might embarrass the first person. These two reasons are my own mind's conclusions.

There are so many differences in this subject. I will summarize them.

Marriage

First, I will answer the most common question I am asked about Egyptian marriage. I have never seen in all my life—neither my mom nor my grandmother—any arranged marriages (forcing someone to marry with no choice to refuse).

Relationships

In the U.S., the couple may have a complete relationship before the wedding day; usually they live together for years before they get married. In Egypt, a complete relationship is never before the wedding day, for Muslims or Christians.

Weddings

In the U.S., the ceremony and the reception are on the same day. In Egypt, you may choose to make the ceremony (*katb elketab*) on a different day. The wife in Egypt doesn't take her husband's last name. Also we don't use last names in Egypt to address people, even if you are the boss; we just use first names with Mr., Miss, or Mrs. before the name.

Financial Responsibilities

In the U.S., the couple usually share everything equally (chores and the family money). In Egypt, the husband is always responsible for the financial life; he should cover everything: the house and the needs of his wife and children, unless the wife chooses to share some of her own money or to support him, if he needs her to. So she doesn't have to pay anything. This is Islamic culture. About the chores, the wife is responsible for it all unless the husband wants to help. This does not derive from Islamic culture.

Divorces

This point always amazes me and it appears so clear that the religion does not always control the culture. Divorce is allowed in Islam; if the couple are not in love or don't understand each other anymore, they can divorce easily. So it is not against the religion in any way. However, the sad point for the divorced person is that it's not easy for the society to accept them 100%, and it is not easy for the divorced person to start a new life. Their opportunity to do this is much less than that of a person with no experience. This is terrible thing, so sad and totally against Islam. In the USA, mostly divorce is against the religion, so people marry within the church and get their divorce within the court. But the divorced person can live a totally normal life, remarry and have a nice new family without a social stigma.

Death

I will never forget my only death experience in the U.S., when my co-worker's mom died and I went to console her and her family. The people were so sad but no tears were shed in front of anyone. I saw smiles. That is something you will never see in Egypt. Also I saw kids of all ages in the place, while in Egypt kids are never around a death event. The place in the USA was so beautiful, full of flowers and pictures of the lost mom, hundreds of them on the shelves, and slide shows. The music was all around the place. The people were dressed very nicely in different colors and different styles. The place was huge. I later discovered that they rented it for the event. All these things you will never see in Egypt. I also learned about embalming, when they take all the blood out of the dead body and pump chemical fluids into it. So the body can last in good condition for weeks, for the funeral and the wake.

Everyone lined up in a long line to get the chance to get into the room to see the deceased. It was very emotional for me even though I never met the woman before she died. Everyone was talking around me about so many different subjects, other than death. My heart was beating so fast and I had a lot of dread, I was trying my best not to show it to anyone. It became more and more difficult when I started to step into the room and got closer to the casket. She was laid out in a beautiful dress and full make up. It was my first time ever to see a dead body. So many wonders and thoughts came to my mind, a lot of emotions and my tears started to come up. I couldn't stop it. How come I would be the only one crying? And I was just about the only one who never met her— that would look so weird. I had to get a handle on my feelings and turned around to go. I went out but had a lot of signs left in my heart and soul after these moments. Things are hard to describe but will live in me, until my own turn will come to leave this world. Something else about death is different in the U.S. It started to spread more in the whole nation recently because it is much cheaper. It is cremation. It means to burn the dead body instead of burial. That is one more thing you will never see in Egypt.

In Egypt, there is total sadness, sorrow and crying for weeks and months. Ladies will wear black for months after the death, sometimes for a whole year. Special people will come to the house in the day of death to wash the dead body and wrap it in white cloth. Just the very close family members are allowed to see the body. They take the body to the mosque to pray for him first, then to the grave in the same day if they can or, at the latest, the next day to bury it under the ground. All the friends, family and neighbors will come to visit the devastated family at their home in the week following the death. Sometimes the family erects a huge tent in which the men console each other, as women usually visit inside the house. Also the family brings a Quran reciter with a beautiful voice to read Quran to everyone through a speaker. That way, with the Quran being recited, everyone around will know there is a death in the neighborhood. Crying and screaming will be heard in the area for a while. Usually the neighbors or the family members will not have any kind of celebration for a while—they consider that disrespectful to the dead. In Islam, we shouldn't scream for death, and we should live our normal lives after three days from the death—or at least try to—except for the widows, whose mourning may last for months. Most of the current Egyptian death cultural practices are far from the Islamic instructions. I have no answer why.

Definitely I would never have been able to evaluate my own culture until I had lived in a different one. Also, I won't be able to see with different eyes until I lived with different people.

7 Interesting Information About My Culture

♦ Egypt is a North African country. It is one of 47 African countries. It is an Arabic country also. It is one of 22 countries that speak Arabic in Africa and Asia.

♦ Arabic is the fifth most spoken language on earth. It is also one of the oldest languages on earth. It is a Semitic language like the Ugaritic, Phoenician, Aramaic, Hebrew, Syriac. There are other nations that adopted the Arabic letters and created their own languages like Farsi, Urdu, Pashto, and Kurdish.

♦ The Arabic alphabet has 28 letters. It is always written in cursive. The Arabic is written and read from right to left, so from an American view the books and documents are read back to front. There are 9 Arabic letters that don't have similar sounds in English, and 2 English letters don't have similar sound in Arabic, *P* and *G*.

♦ 15 letters of the Arabic alphabet have dots now. Arabic was originally written without dots above or below. The dots have been introduced more recently. I am so glad that happened way before I was born. You will never imagine how hard it would be without dots, until you know Arabic. We have many letters with the same shape, but you can tell the difference between them only with the dots. Like, ث ت ب, the dots make you realize the difference in the sounds. How could they tell the difference in the sounds without dots? I have no idea!

♦ The English language consists of many words with Arabic origin, such as checkmate, cotton, magazine, algebra, mummy, sherbet, sugar, tuna, and alcohol.

♦ Arabic has a linguistic system totally different from European languages. Words are constructed from a three letter "root" which conveys an idea. Letters are then added in and around the root to create words. This makes Arabic a vocabulary rich language. It is actually one of the richest languages. An example for how rich is this language, in English there is just one word to say "lion." In Arabic, there are 300 words that mean lion. Each word describes the lion with different way, depending on how the lion looks, feels, moves, acts, etc. So each word of the 300 will give you different meaning about the lion. As an example, instead of saying, "I saw a lion cub," you will say, "I saw *shebl*." Arabic is my first language, but I still don't know all of these words. I guess the old Arabs respected the lion so much. Another example for how rich Arabic is that, in English, you have 5 words to describe how much you love someone. In Arabic there are about 53 words that you can use to describe exactly with details, just in one word, how do you feel toward someone.

- Arabic literature has a great old history. It goes back 16 centuries. The earliest form of Arabic literature is poetry. Arabic poetry is very special in history, and in my heart. Arabic poetry always has good meaning, full of wisdom or philosophy in a steady beat, with words full of music and harmony. You can tell I am in love with it.

- There are two Arabic versions. *Classical Arabic* is the official language. It is used in school teaching, writing, books, and newspapers. It never changes. *Modern Arabic* is used in daily spoken contexts. Each Arabic country has its own, with its own accent, but Arabic people from different countries mostly can understand each other.

- In Egypt, kids never leave their parents' house at any age until their marriage day. Both boys and girls are the same; they never leave unless temporarily, for studying in a different city or country, and that is not common. After they finish, they come back to their parents' house. Also, their parents usually are responsible for them financially at any age, until they are married and have their own house.

- In Egypt, it is a big cause of shame if one of your parents or both are old or sick and you leave them to live by themselves. Even in a nursing home or seniors' place. One of the biggest shames you might think about! I know it is totally different here, and it is very normal for that to happen.

- In Egypt, we don't use last names to call anyone in the whole country, except the president. At work, schools, anywhere, even for teachers and principals, we use the first name with Mr. or Miss in the front. Also we don't take the husband's last name after marriage. All the Arabic names have meanings. One more thing about names: I noticed here some families' last names may be used as girls' names, which you will never see in Egypt.

- Approximately 90% of Egyptians are Muslim (primarily Sunni), 9% are Christian Coptic orthodox and 1% are other Christians.

- Egypt's population is around 90,000,000. 98% of them live on 4% of the Egyptian land, around the river Nile. The rest of the land is desert.

- Ancient Egyptian women had more rights and privileges than most other women in the ancient world. For example, they could own property, carry out business deals, and initiate divorce. Women from wealthy families could become doctors or priestesses.

- The shape of ancient Egyptian pyramids is thought to have been inspired by the spreading rays of the sun.

- The famous Great Pyramid at Giza was built as a burial place for King Khufu (2589 – 2566 B.C.) and took more than 20 years to build. It was built from over two million limestone blocks, each one weighing as much as two and a half elephants. It stands about 460 feet (149 m) high—taller than the Statue of Liberty. The base of the Great Pyramid takes up almost as much space as five football fields.

♦ Ramses II (1279 – 1212 B.C.) is often considered the greatest pharaoh (*great house*) of the Egyptian empire. He ruled Egypt for 60 years and was the only pharaoh to carry the title "the Great" after his name. He had over 90 children: approximately 56 boys and 40 girls. He had eight official wives and nearly 100 concubines. He also had red hair, which was associated with the god Seth.

♦ The life expectancy of Egyptians in 2013 was 72.12 years, which ranked 120th in the world. The life expectancy of males is 69.56 years and 74.81 years for females. Japan had the world's highest life expectancy at 84 years old. The United States was the 34th, with a life expectancy of 79 years. Here I have to share that the Egyptians usually feel like more than 80 years old when they are just at 60, even if they are healthy. The retirement age in Egypt is 60 years old. This might be a reason for feeling old early, especially since 95% of the retired people in Egypt have no plans for their life after their retirement.

♦ It is very rare for any man or women over 30 years old to change their work career or study college again in a different field, even if they hate their current one.

♦ In all my life in Egypt and all my family's life, we have never heard about arranged marriage. This culture is in some places in India, but people always ask me about it.

♦ The other common question for me here is "Do you sleep and always wear your Hijab (cover) at home?"

The answer in definitely, "No." Also this part gets confused with some Sikhs' cultures.

♦ Cousins' marriage is very common in Egypt and other Arab countries. It is usually after a love story. No matter first, second or third cousins, it is common in all. I was shocked to discover that cousins' marriage is illegal in some states here.

8   True or False, Rumors About Me

I have no doubt that you know yourself very well. No one on earth would know you better than yourself! You might feel that some like you, love you, or even hate you, but you will never be able to see how exactly they see you. It might seem impossible for you, but not for me.

I am not seen as a totally normal human being in this world, but rather as a Muslim who wears Hijab and lives in a non-Muslim majority country. It's not because I am different; in the U.S., everyone is different somehow. It's because I belong to a religion that is frequently misrepresented. Also, it is the only religion that gets all the negative news in the media. So people who I don't know personally see me as a reflection of what they hear about my religion in the regular media or social media or from their friends who might spread rumors.

It's really hard to discuss why that usually happens, but I can tell how that personally happened during my life in the U.S.

I have many friends who are non-Muslims, and because I am so open to hear questions about my religion from anyone, they feel comfortable asking me about what they hear, to find out if it's true or false. I am thankful for them; it's because of their questions I am sharing my answers with the world in this book.

Committing Suicide

My American friend came to have dinner with me one day. I was preparing the food when she said, "Rania, I want to ask you about something I read about Islam on Facebook. I felt it was really offensive, but I want to ask you about it. May I?"

"Sure you may!" I said.

She said that she read a joke with this meaning:

> *Don't forget to mark your calendars. As you may already know, it is a sin for a Muslim male to see any woman other than his wife naked and if he does, he must commit suicide. So next Saturday at 1:00 P.M. Eastern Time, all American women are asked to walk out of their house completely naked to help weed out any neighborhood terrorists. Circling your block for one hour is recommended for this anti-terrorist effort.*

Then she said, "Is this really in Islam, that the man has to commit suicide if he saw a naked women?"

I smiled and said, "No! Not at all! Committing suicide is one of the worst things to do in Islam. It actually takes the person out of the religion, according to Islamic teachings. Seeing a naked women who is not his wife is a sin that a Muslim has to repent and ask forgiveness from God. He will get this forgiveness, then is all done."

This rumor actually is proof that Muslims who are terrorists are not real Muslims and are not practicing Islam. Whether or not Muslims are offended by female nudity is a moot point—clearly the terrorists aren't. An examination of the activities of the hijackers in the days and months leading to the September 11 attacks shows that at least some of them "enjoyed naked lap dancers in Daytona Beach" (Palm Beach Post). Not just September 11 hijackers, also the terrorist who committed the Charlie Hebdo attack, and a couple of those who did the November 2015 attack in Paris, actually had drugs and liquor as well as girlfriends. All of these acts are forbidden for those who practice the religion of Islam. Terrorists are not Muslims who practice the real Islam.

The Bible

I worked with a beautiful Hispanic lady in her 60s. I enjoyed treating her like my mom because of the huge amount of kindness and care that she had in her heart. One day she asked, "Rania, can I ask you a question about your religion?"

"Sure you can!" I replied.

"I have a friend who told me that if a Muslim gets a Bible, he has to be killed in Islam. I don't know any other Muslim but you, and I really don't know if what she said is true or not?"

"This is not true at all! And my proof is that I am a Muslim who practices Islam, and I actually have a Bible in my house. I'm still alive. Also, I grew up in a Muslim majority country, and I always saw the Bible in the public libraries," I said.

"Thank you, Rania! Now, I can go and correct my friend," she said with a big smile on her beautiful face.

No Love

I was checking my emails when I saw one from an American Muslim friend. The email was forwarded from a leader at an Episcopal Church. They were searching for a Muslim who was willing to go give classes at the church about Islam. The email was very interesting—a church and a class about Islam! I checked with my friend about the email, and she told me her co-worker was a member of that church. They contacted her because she was the only Muslim he knew.

My friend told me, "I know you are interested about reading about different religions, and you write articles about Islam, so I thought of you."

I got really busy after this conversation with her, so I didn't respond to the email to ask about more details as I had been planning to. Days, weeks, and couple of months passed.

One day in February, I checked the news and learned about the three young Muslims who were killed in Chapel Hill, N.C. I was so sad that happened, and I was sure the killer did that because he was a victim of Islamophobia. I started to feel really worried about my children's future as American Muslims. I was thinking how could I help people understand me and my children more? Then, I remembered the email that I got a few months ago. I felt so guilty for not responding to this email. I thought sharing the truth about my religion will surely destroy the rumors, increase the understanding, and maybe even stop another hate crime from happening. I got my laptop and sent an email to the sender asking for more details.

She replied back and we decided to meet and talk about the details at the mall. She was a beautiful, nice blond lady in her 40s. She sat by me, and we talked. I asked her why she decided to host classes about Islam in her church. She answered, "I had a situation with my sister last Thanksgiving that led me to do that. I invited many friends who were from different religions and backgrounds, and my sister was with me preparing for the day. I told her we have to make sure we have some vegetarian food because there are some Muslims and Hindus who are coming. (She thought Muslims don't eat meat, which is not right). My sister looked at me angrily and asked, *Really? Will you bring Muslims into your house?* "Yes, I will! What is the problem?" *These people don't have the word love in their holy book. You shouldn't let those people in your house,* my sister said.

Then the lady said to me, "I was so sad that was my own sister's reaction about Muslims. I really don't know any information about the Islamic faith. I was talking at my church with some friends who told me they don't either, and we all decided we should know more. One of our church's members said he had a Muslim co-worker, so I contacted her."

I was listening to her words with a lot of appreciation for her courage to seek knowledge and to deal with the negative information she heard. Sadly, not many people would think to do that in our world! I became very excited to start these classes with these amazing people who were from different religions and backgrounds, and I spent a great time giving them five classes about Islam.

I talked with them, not as a scholar because I'm definitely not one, but as a regular Muslim who loves her religion, loves all the people around her, and really wants everyone to understand her through her behavior and through the true sources of her religion. I shared with them all the information they, as non-Muslims, should know about me and answered all their questions. One piece of information I shared with them was that the word love is mentioned 83 times in the Quran.

The "M" Word

This situation was the one that affected me the most of all. Not because of the rumors and the lies it contained, but because of the way someone had so much hatred in his heart to create it.

My American friend who is not Muslim was visiting me one day and said, "I think I did something good today that you will like." "What?" I asked.

"I got an email from someone I know, about Muslims. I thought the email was very offensive and I couldn't even finish reading it. The beginning of the email said these words were written by Jeff Foxworthy. And because I doubted Jeff would write these words, I went online to check if he was really the person who wrote these offensive words. I found out that he didn't write any of these words. So, I sent back to my friend that this email was very offensive and full of rumors and not even by Jeff Foxworthy. And I attached the link for her."

I really was happy that I had this great friend. And thanked her so much for her amazing response. I really wanted to see that email. I asked her to send it to me, and I read it. Everything in that email, which I will share, was totally wrong. Nothing was even close to being true. I have seen things similar to this before, but what caught my eyes the most in this email was the ending. This person who made up this email wanted to make sure that anyone who has no information about Islam will spread his lies to everyone in his list. Here's the email:

> The "M" Word by Jeff Foxworthy
>
> Have you ever wondered why it's okay to make jokes about Catholics, the Pope, Jews, Christians, the Irish, the Italians, the Polish, the Chinese, the French (including French Canadians), the elderly, bad golfers, men / women, blacks / whites, husbands, wives, etc, but it's "politically incorrect" and very insensitive to make jokes about Muslims? Well, folks it's time to level the playing field and be

politically correct by including the Muslims, too! Jeff Foxworthy on Muslims:

> *If you grow, refine and sell heroin for a living, but you have a moral objection to liquor, You may be a Muslim.*

> *If you own a $3,000 machine gun and a $5,000 rocket launcher, but you can't afford shoes, You may be a Muslim.*

> *If you have more wives than teeth, You may be a Muslim.*

> *If you wipe your butt with your bare hand but consider bacon to be unclean, You may be a Muslim.*

> *If you think vests come in two styles: Bullet-proof and suicide, You may be a Muslim.*

> *If you can't think of anyone you haven't declared jihad against, You may be a Muslim.*

> *If you consider television dangerous but routinely carry explosives in your clothing, You may be a Muslim.*

> *If you were amazed to discover that cell phones have uses other than setting off roadside bombs, You may be a Muslim.*

> *If you have nothing against women and think every man should own, at least, four, You may be a Muslim.*

*If you find this offensive and don't forward it, you
are part of the growing problem in America! If you
find this "politically distasteful" and delete it, then
perhaps you, too, are a Muslim.*

Now, I have to admit, it's not easy to read something like that
about myself. I am Muslim who spent many years of my life in
Muslim countries and have many Muslim friends from all over the
world. I am someone who practices Islam as much as I can. The
only two sources of Islam are, God's words (Quran) and Prophet
Muhammad's (peace be upon him) actions and sayings (sunnah),
and that is it. Any Islamic scholar who would say something that
doesn't match these two sources or against any of them would be
out of the religion. It's that simple! So there is no chance that a
Muslim would do any of these things in this nonsense email
because he is a Muslim. So proving that all these things are not
Islamic is very simple and easy.

But the issue is why would someone think that way? Why
would he make something false about someone or any religion and
call it a joke? Why would he end it in a way that will encourage
ignorant people to spread it to even more people and create more
fear and hatred in the world for me and for my children? These are
questions that I have no answers for.

On The Train

On the train to downtown Chicago in 2005, Person 1 boarded
and sat down. After two stops, Persons 2 and 3 got on the train,
and they started to look around for empty seats. Then they found
two by Person 1. Persons 2 and 3 seemed like friends. They started

to talk about many different subjects and then their conversation turned to politics.

Person 2 said, "Do you know why we should get rid of all the Muslims in the USA?"

Person 3 "Why?"

Person 2 "They are just evil people."

Person 1 was listening to the conversation and got mad at the way Person 2 was talking. He was an Arab Muslim, but he didn't look like one. He thought about interrupting the conversation to stop him, but he was too scared to tell them he was a Muslim. Person 2 especially seemed aggressive, and he might start a fight with him if he knew he was a Muslim. He decided to keep quiet (a typical reaction from an Arab).

Person 3 said, "But I don't think all of them are evil. Maybe some are not." Person 2 responded, "All of them are evil. I even have proof for you. They all believe in a holy book. I think they call it Qureen or Korain something like that. In their holy book, it said that they should kill all the Americans. 9/11 was just the start." At this point, Person 1 couldn't take it anymore. He turned to face them and said, "Excuse me, sir, but nothing you said about Muslims and their holy book was true."

Person 2 asked with a grumpy face, "How did you know?"

Person 1 said, "Because I am a Muslim. My holy book's name is the Quran. I suggest you get one from any mosque and read it, before you spread any wrong information about it and about me." Person 1 was really worried about Person 2's reaction, so he decided to get up and move to another seat as fast as he could. After he got up, he turned back and said, "By the way, the Quran was on earth 1100 years before America's existence. This is the number one proof for you that what you said was not true." Then, he disappeared between the crowds in the train.

Person 1 went home and was so nervous about what he did. He was so worried because he might see Person 2 again on the train any other day. They both ride the train every day to work. Days passed. Person 1 noticed that Person 2 always gave him weird looks on the train. He got even more nervous. That lasted for a couple of months.

One day, Person 1 felt someone was tapping on his shoulder. He turned to see who, and he saw it was Person 2. Person 1 was shocked and didn't say a word.

Person 2 said, "Hi, do you remember me?"

Person 1 said with a nervous voice, "Not really."

Person 2 said, "I am the one who was spreading bad information about you and your religion on the train."

Person 1 said, "Yes, I remember."

Person 2 said, "I spent the past months reading the Quran and reading about Islamic history, and I found out that everything I thought about your religion and everything I said about it was totally wrong. I stopped you now to say that I am really sorry for every word I said."

Just imagine if Person 1 decided to move to be away when he started to hear things he didn't like, or if he decided to be quiet for the whole time because of his fears. I think that Person 2 would keep spreading his wrong information to Persons 3 and 4, and 4 will spread it to 5 and 6, and so it will keep going.

Now you need to know that Person 1 was my husband.

Dear Muslims: Be positive, talk with people, answer their questions, and break your fears.

Dear haters: Read to know the truth.

I know for sure there are many other rumors and lots of false information about my religion out there that hasn't reached me yet, but I believe that the good is still greater than the bad in our world, and I have faith that love will prevail. That's why I will never lose hope and will keep trying to spread true knowledge as much as I can. Also, I will always make sure of anything I hear against anyone and check it from the right sources to know whether it's true or false.

9 From One World to Another

I heard one of the most annoying sounds coming from very far away. It was getting closer and closer and closer, louder and louder and louder! Then, I opened my eyes, and I realized it was my alarm clock.

It was time for me to get up and be ready for my first day at my new school as a high school student. I was so excited and nervous at the same time. I was hoping for nice, good teachers, and hoping for kind, friendly classmates.

In Egyptian public schools, we study six years in elementary co-ed schools, then we move to middle school for three years, then high school for three years. Middle school and high school are separate for boys or for girls. College education is co-ed again.

From One World to Another

In all my educational life, I had very good relationships with my teachers. I always was trying to do my best in the class, finish my homework on time and study hard for tests and quizzes. I also was trying to earn their respect and to learn from them as much as I could. At that time, I had a typical Egyptian definition for what a bad student was. In my mind, they were the ones who couldn't answer the teachers' questions right and got the worst grades in the class. I thought those were the bad students who didn't care about learning. They usually liked to sit in the back of the class, so the teachers would not call on them. I never knew at that time, they might not have had the ability to learn or they might have had social problems stopping them from being good students.

In my first day of high school, I entered my huge new school. The school was old and very close to the Mediterranean seashore. I was hoping that my class would be on the side that I had a view of the sea. I went to the office, and I got my class number. It was on the second floor at the end of the hall.

After I found my class, the first thing I checked was the windows. I was so happy when I found out that my dream had come true and I would be able to see the beautiful view all year long. I picked my desk, the one closest to the window. It was an old wooden one with many writings and marks on it. I sat down and waited, and thought, *Who will come in and sit by me? A nice girl, a smart one, a mean girl, or one of the bad girls?* After a couple of minutes, a girl entered the class who sat by me and later became one of my best friends and she is still my friend until this moment. After the class was complete we had the schedule for the school year. Many of the subjects were totally new for me, but I was so ready to start.

From One World to Another

In that year I had experiences that happened to me for the first time ever. It was with my Arabic teacher. She was a tall woman who was very quiet. She used to wear very simple and very covered clothes, even though she was not wearing Hijab. She always had her hair up the same way, and never took care of her looks, like other normal young women in her age would.

Every time she taught something, she said something wrong about the lesson. In the beginning I wasn't sure what to do? Should I raise my hand and tell her the information was wrong? I wondered how she would react to me. I worried about that for many days. Every time, I could hardly control myself from raising my hand and telling her about her mistakes.

One day, I couldn't take it anymore. I told myself, I would tell her nicely, not in the front of everyone, and make sure that I would be polite, so she shouldn't be mad at me. I collected all my courage; I waited until she was alone in the classroom, and told her about her mistakes. She smiled and said, "Oh yes, you are right Rania. Thank you." I took a deep breath; I was relieved. She was fine, not mad at me. However, after that day her mistakes continued.

I never stopped thinking about what to do. I only had two choices. I could either ignore her mistakes to keep her respect, or I could keep telling her about her mistakes during the class. In the latter case, I'd help my friends to learn the right information, but I might lose her respect forever.

My choice was the second one. When one of my friends raised her hand and asked a question, the teacher answered her question with the completely wrong answer. I lost her love on that day by correcting her answer, but I realized something: there is something wrong with the Egyptian Education system. How come this woman who was never able to control the class well, and taught with so many mistakes could be a teacher? Actually that thought was enough to lead my future away from education, and this is what made me believe that teaching is the most important job ever! If a doctor can affect your sickness, and if an engineer can affect a building, a teacher's personality can affect the future of an entire generation.

In the Egyptian education system, the teacher is the one who has total responsibility for the class, even if the class has a lot of students (forty or more). I think the relationship between the teacher and the students in the public Egyptian schools is very similar to stories I heard long ago about the relationship between teachers and students here in a Catholic school.

The students wear a uniform to school every day. It shouldn't be too open or too short. The girls cannot wear any kind of make-up or even come to school with the leftovers of the last night's make-up on their faces.

They can't come to school with nail polish, or have their hair down. The teachers usually need to be so strict and firm, so the students will not walk over them. Teachers, most of the time, are either tough, with a strong personality so they can control the class, or so nice and kind that they never raise their voices. Then the class will be loud and out of control.

When I came to the USA, I had the chance to see the American education system after my son started school. I volunteered at his school a couple of times. From the first moment, I dreamed about working in this system. Especially after I spent few minutes in this class.

I watched how the teachers were dealing with the students, and that was what attracted me the most. Not the three teachers with fewer than 20 students, nor the beautiful, colorful, nicely decorated classroom. It was how the teacher was talking with the students, and how she was dealing with all of them, the smart and not so smart, the talented and not so talented. Her ability to control the class with a smile on her face was most impressive. She even gave them some freedom to talk or move without losing their attention or respect for her.

I longed, that day, to go back and I attend all my school years here in the USA. And guess what? My dream came true! I worked as a teacher's aide in Special Education years after that day. At that time, I had the opportunity to attend, with my students, so many different classes in different grades from preschool to high school.

I have a lot of respect and love in my heart toward my good teachers in Egypt. I learned from them. They encouraged me to improve and do my best.

I totally understand all the elements which may hinder the Egyptian education system from achieving a high educational level. So many factors may play a role, like the numbers of students in the classes and the ability to get a teacher's aide to help if needed, plus the financial problems. I can also think of the excuses for the bad teachers I had in my life in Egypt. I don't think the problems were in themselves, but in the system which couldn't help them to pick the right job to match their abilities and their personalities.

The first thing that came to my mind, when I was asked about what I thought is missing in the American education system, was that it doesn't have a second language program for the elementary and secondary students.

This is a missed opportunity because there are a great number of people from different countries and cultures, who speak many different languages in the United States. The students would have ample opportunities to practice the second language, and it could be a key that would open many doors in the students' lives. With a second language, careers would open for them in the U.S. and throughout the world.

One day I had training at my work, and it was about English language learners. The lecturer explained how good it is to help the bilingual students learn in their own languages. She said also that learning two languages or more in early childhood can increase the brain's ability to think, learn and create.

One of the best benefits I got from the Egyptian Educational system was my English as a second language, and I chose French as a third language from among German and Spanish.

Being a part of the Egyptian and American educational systems from different positions—as a student, a teacher and a parent—gave me the chance to see both of them from the inside and outside; also to feel the advantages and disadvantages of both systems.

All my experiences in the Egyptian education system affected my personality, mostly in a positive way. My educational years in Egypt helped me to learn more about the world, plus my own country. The American Education system showed me a new kind of relationship that can be created between the teacher and the students. It opened my eyes on a new beautiful world. I've been learning from it every day.

❖

10 My Crazy Wish

At one point in my life, reaching the moon with my own hands was closer than me having a job in schools. In Egypt, when I was in high school, being a teacher was the farthest thing from my mind to do in life. The reason was that I really wanted to do something different from what my family had done. My mom was a teacher, then she became a high school principal for many years. My dad also had worked as a tutor for a long time. Both of my parents and five of my aunts and cousins were teachers. Even though I was a good student all my life and I enjoyed teaching my younger brother, I didn't want to spend the rest of my life in a school; I needed to be different.

In Egypt, the students don't usually choose what they love to do in life. The students wait for their high school final results, and depending on the total grade they get, they would have some choices for their future career. Students usually choose what might help them to have a good income, rather than what they really like to do. My high school grades were good.

As a result, I had more than six fields to choose one of them for my career, such as, education, commerce, law, science. My family tried to convince me that I would be a good teacher, but my answer was "impossible." I chose commerce to be as far as I could from teaching. I decided to specialize in business administration in my last two years of college. I earned my bachelor's degree. I thought it was the beginning, but I didn't know, that was the end of that career with me forever.

When I came to the United States, I struggled a lot to be a part of the community and to make friends. Being able to talk with people was hard because of my bad English, so having a job one day was not an easy wish to achieve. When my first son started school, I decided to volunteer in his school.

The first time there, I was amazed about the huge differences between an American education and an Egyptian education. How the teacher was dealing with all the students through their different educational levels, for example, was different. How much fun the students were having in the class was also different. Honestly, I wished, that day, I were a child with my son in that classroom. I thought that was just a crazy wish, but later happened.

The second time I had a chance to go for a tour in the school. It was small old building. The walls were full of beautiful, colorful pictures and posters. All of the staff were very friendly and their faces were bright with beautiful smiles. It was a place that you have to wish to be a part of. My eyes went to one of the teachers' ID card. It had the school name and her name on it. I thought for a second, *Could I have one of these IDs one day with my own name on it?* I woke from the daydream and said to myself, *How would you work in an American school when you don't have a degree in education? Even if you had a degree, English is your second language. Don't go far with your dreams!*

In that school I met one of the staff members; a nice young woman who became my best friend later. I told her about my dream. She guided me for the WorkKeys Assessment Test, to apply as a teacher's aide in any school. I was so happy to hear about this hope that would take me closer to my dream.

I worked hard to find a college, then I worked harder for months to pass the tests. Finally I got the approval. I was able to fill out applications for jobs for the new school year. I applied to more than five schools around my area. I waited and waited for a long time, but no one called me for an interview. I started to lose my hope again but, right before I reached that point, I got a phone call.

It was a beautiful sunny day in August. I was with my best friend, showing her how to cook a famous Egyptian dish, when the phone rang. I picked the phone up; it was my husband. He told me that I got a phone call from a principal today and he said I would have an interview the following week. I took a deep breath and said, "Are you joking or talking seriously?" He said, "I swear that happened three minutes ago." Then he said, "You didn't ask me what school it is." I said, "Oh, yes! What school is it?" He said, "I think your dream is so close to being true." It was my son's old school. That was the purest moment of happiness for me. For the whole week, my friend worked with me to practice how to perform well in an American interview. And I was ready!

I was so nervous and worried. My friend said I had to show confidence in the interview and try to say that I am perfect. But I knew that I am not, because English is my second language. My heartbeats were so fast when I was getting closer to the door to enter the interview. I went in; it was a conference room.

The principal was setting on my right hand and two blond women on my left. They welcomed me, and the principal started to ask me all the interview questions. Then he asked, "What do you think are your weak points?" My friend told me not to answer with anything negative about me in this question, but I couldn't. I looked at him and said, "English is my second language, but I am trying my best to improve it every day." He smiled and said, "Thank you! There are two more people applying for this position; I will call you tomorrow to tell you who will get it." I remember that the best comment I received was from the two ladies' eyes and smiles. One of them said, "It was really nice meeting you, Rania." I went home and couldn't wait to receive the phone call the next day.

The next day I got the call; it was the principal. He said I didn't get the job because one of the other applicants had a teaching degree, so she got the teacher's aide job. Then he said, "They need an aide for Special Education and I gave the coordinator your application and she will call you soon." I barely could say *Thank you*, Because tears started to pour down my face, and I couldn't control myself from crying. My tears were not because I didn't get the job; they were because I didn't get this particular job in this school, which I wished one day to have. Then I lost my dream, when it was really within reach.

A couple of days after that, I got a phone call from the Special Education coordinator. I was interviewed the same day. The next day I got a job, but at a different school. It was a school for pre-K, kindergarten and first grade. I was helping a student in kindergarten, but I got the chance to spend so much time in all the grades. Three months later my student moved. I was asked to change my position to a classroom in a different school, because their aide moved out the state. I asked what school? The answer was *my dream school*.

My Crazy Wish

Finally I was a part of the school, after so many unexpected changes. My happiness when I had my school ID equaled my happiness when I had my bachelor's degree, or even more. I spent two of my favorite work years in that school. Even my crazy wish came true. I got the chance to be in all the grades starting from pre-K and up to high school and college. I was able to attend, learn, and enjoy being an aide for the students and a student for myself in all the grades.

I have learned from my experience that it is not important to think about how far or hard it is to reach your dream. Instead, the most important thing is to take the first step toward it.

11   Unforgettable Moments:
The Swimming Suit

I opened my eyes on that morning with great happiness. I was so excited for the next hours to pass and reach that moment. Finally I would see him and hold him in my embrace after three years of missing him and longing for him. I couldn't wait to see how he looked and what changed in him. He was always nervous and uncomfortable traveling overseas, between Egypt and the US for around 20 hours. It was not easy at all for him to make that decision. I couldn't believe that my dad finally accepted my invitation to visit me in the U.S. *Finally he will see my home, spend time with me and my family, and I will talk and talk with him for hours, just like our old happy days*, I thought.

I arrived at the airport and looked at the arrival gate, waiting to let his face's features bring out a smile from my heart. I saw his kind, tired face coming out from the gate, looking everywhere to see someone he knows. He took a deep breath when he saw me and I ran to him calling him loudly, "Dad!! I missed you!!" I spent beautiful seconds in his hug before we retrieved his luggage and left the airport. He looked so different! He had many wrinkles on his face and he had lost so much weight. It was my first time ever seeing my dad as an old man. I was so worried that he was ill and hiding that from me, as my family always does with any bad news.

After I made sure he was fine and the weight he had lost was not the effect of any illness, I wondered how I could make him happy and help him enjoy his time in the U.S.! I made many plans, and since he stayed from spring through the summer, those plans were not hard to make in Chicago.

I remember the day when he woke up on a March morning, stood by the window and called me loudly, "Rania come here now!" "Yes, Dad, are you OK?" I wondered. "Rania, what is that?" he said pointing to outside the window, looking surprised. I smiled and said, "It is snow, Dad." "Do you get snow in the spring?" he asked with wonder. "Yes, Dad, we do!" I answered. He started shivering and said, "I feel cold." "Dad, there is no way you are cold. The heat is on, and it is 70 degrees inside the house," I said, thinking that he might be kidding. He looked at me seriously and said, "Rania, please bring me something with long sleeves to wear. Just looking at that snow made me feel really cold." I brought him what he asked me for and I thought that I had to excuse him; this was his first time ever to see real snow coming down from the sky, and he knew it was below freezing outside the house, and he was always cold in the Egyptian winter, with rain and 50 degrees Fahrenheit.

After a couple of months, it was the 4th of July and the city had a big carnival, so I took my dad there. He was so happy and spent a nice day, but I will never forget his comment after the day: "Oh, Rania, these American people are so nice and friendly, they have been smiling at me all the time and offering me things. I never thought of them like that from what I always hear about America from the Egyptian news." "You are right, Dad, sometimes what you see is actually the opposite of what you hear," I said.

One day I thought about a place that my dad might like and we all might enjoy in the summer, so the water park sounded like a great idea. We all love swimming, and my kids would have fun. I told everyone about the plan for the next day. They all were very happy and excited for the water park, and I was on the top of the list since swimming is one of my favorite things to do. We checked the weather, and it was sunny and perfect for the fun day. We got everything ready for the outing: food, swimming suits and clothes, then we all had a happy exciting night anticipating our trip.

The next morning we all wore our swimming suits and went to the water park. Before we went to buy our tickets, I remembered something that stopped me for a minute. I remembered that day when I went with my husband to a swimming pool right after I decided to wear my Hijab, so I wore my covered swimming suit that covers all my body with the same material like any regular swimming suit. After I started to swim in  the pool, the manager came to me and said, "Excuse me ma'am, you can't swim here with what you are wearing!" I asked why. He said, "It looks like regular clothes and that is not allowed in this swimming pool" I tried to explain to him that it was a swimming suit, not regular clothes, but he didn't get it, so I sadly left the pool that day.

When I remembered that situation and how embarrassed I was, I decided to check with the water park's manager before I bought the tickets, to make sure that my swimming suit was just fine to use in this water park. So I asked the cashier, who called the manager. He was a tall man with brown hair and green eyes. I looked at him, smiled and said, "Hi, I have a question for you." "Yes!!" he said. "I am wearing my swimming suit and I just want to make sure it's okay for me to use the park with my family and my kids." He looked at me and said, "Sorry. You will not be able to use the water park with these clothes!" "It is not clothes, it is a swimming suit with the same material and the basic design for any regular swimming suit," I said with my disappointed face. "This is one of the rules here. I am sorry, you can't use the park," he said firmly. I told him, "Okay, I won't use the water, so we will just pay for the rest of my family to use the park, right?" "Sorry, you have to pay for a ticket for yourself, also, if you will enter the park anyway," he said. "Even if I won't use the water at all?" I asked "Yes!" he said.

My husband didn't like the way the man was talking to me, so he said, "Let's go somewhere else, Rania." I remembered how happy and excited my dad was and my kids were for the water park and I said, "No, we don't have to go somewhere else. If this is the rule then, I am OK. We will pay and I won't use the park. I want my dad and my kids to have fun." We bought the tickets for everyone including me and we entered the park.

It was early in the morning the park was not crowded at all. Then gradually more people started to come. My dad didn't really play as I expected him to do. He was tired and asked to sit after a little bit. I felt so bad that my husband had to go wait in a long line for each slide with one of our kids, then he would stand in the whole line again for the same slide for our other kid. *If I could go with him, I would save so much effort and time for him, and the boys will get to use more rides*, I thought. While we were moving from one slide to another, I noticed something in the water, something that changed everything in my feelings on that day.

12   Unforgettable Moments:
Justice

I called my husband and my dad. "Do you see what I see?" I asked them, looking at a man who was playing in the water with his kids. That man was wearing a cotton T-shirt, very much considered *regular clothes*.

"Yes, I see him, but maybe no one noticed him, Rania. If they see him, they may ask him to leave the water!" my husband said. I looked to my husband and said, "Really, don't you see all these lifeguards everywhere around. They actually are looking at him now, but no one asked him not to use the water park."

"It's okay. Rania, I came here for the kids. Let's go to a different slide and forget about that," said my dad, trying to calm me down. But I started to get mad after that moment. I was wearing swimming suit material, and how come I couldn't use the park but that man who was wearing cotton could enjoy the day? I listened to my husband and my dad and just moved with them to a different slide.

There, I saw three different people who were wearing regular clothes (T-shirts and even shorts) playing and using the water. At the same moment I saw the manager walking on the other side of that slide. I left everyone and quickly ran to him. I tried to be calm and said, "Excuse me, Mister! I am glad you are here right now. Do you see all these people who are in the water wearing all kinds of regular clothes?" I pointed to the water while talking to him.

"Oh, yes!! If any of the lifeguards see them, he sure will ask them to leave the water!" he said, turned around and left me right away. I went back to my family. I was mad, and told them about what he said. They tried to calm me down again but I was extremely disappointed. The hours passed and everything was the same. Everyone else was enjoying the park with their families, including those who had street clothes on, except me.

After a couple of hours, my son was crying because he wanted me to go with him in one of the slides while my husband was with my other son on a different slide. I kept telling my son, "No!" and he kept crying. Then I saw that man again. I told my dad, "Please watch my son, I will be back!" My dad saw the anger in my eyes and heard it in my voice and said, "Rania, please don't get yourself into trouble. I don't want this man to do something else to you. Maybe he hates Muslims!" I didn't respond, but instead walked straight to the manager and said with all my anger, "Do you think this is fair? How come I am the only one who is not allowed to use the park and I am sure that I was the only one who asked about the rules to follow? How come everyone else is having fun with their family but me? Is it because I wanted to respect the place?"

The man was shocked at how angry I was, and hopefully he was thinking of everything I said, "Yes, you are right about that!" he said. "We are sorry for what happened to you today, and we will give you back all the money you paid for yourself and your family. You all can stay and spend the rest of the day after the refund, but I'm sorry you still won't be able to use the water." "Thank you!" I said. I hadn't expect he would do anything for me. I went back to my dad in a different mood. I was proud of myself that I did something. I was positive! I had expressed myself, and the manager responded to my words. I didn't get to use the water, but at least my family used it for free!

I went home that night with many different feelings. It is just hard to describe all of them in words! I couldn't understand then why this man acted that way toward me. After I came back, I contacted my American friends and told them proudly about my story and how I got the money back. The next day I told my American friend, who was my neighbor also. Her reaction was not expected at all, and what she did was even beyond my thoughts.

13 Unforgettable Moments:
A Treasure

I was smiling, telling her the story, when she looked at me with a serious face and said "Really, Rania!! Are you happy to get the money back and that is it?"

"What do you mean?" I asked. She continued, "I mean this man should allow you to use the park and give you a free pass for the whole season for saying don't use it. How dare he say no, for you to use the park? I am so mad that he did. You need to give me the name of that place, and I will call them to complain."

I was shocked at everything she said. I never thought of that at all. I was thinking I did good arguing with him, and getting the ticket money refunded. This is one thing not all of Muslims or Arabs who were born in the Middle East will do. We mostly would rather be quiet than ask for our rights (which might lead to trouble). One of the famous idioms in my culture is, *He who is always afraid is always safe.*

So what I did was more than what I thought I could ever do, and what she was saying was more than I could imagine. I told her the name of the place, then I had to leave. I went back to my house. I spent the night with my family while I was thinking of everything she said.

The next day was a regular day. My husband went to his work, and my dad and my kids were sleeping, when I heard an unexpected knock on my door. "Who could come now with no notice?" I thought. I opened the door to see who that was. It was my neighbor. I was so worried when I saw her. Her face was red, and she looked so mad and sad. "Are you okay?" I asked nervously.

"No!" she answered. "What's wrong?" I asked. "I just came from the water park that you went to," she said. "What? Why did you go there?" I wondered. "To fight for you and your family," she said. I was stunned for a second, then I asked her, "What happened to make you go all the way there? You said you would call them?"

"I called them many times, asking for the manager, to complain and they didn't connect me to him. I was so frustrated, I decided to go myself to meet him there. I went there, asked for him and told him, "I am very mad because we have wonderful neighbors who are very good people and you prevented them from enjoying their day here in the park just because the mom is covered!!"

Then she continued, "That man was so mean and said this is the rule, and I gave them their money back!" Then I started to fight with him, that what he did for you was not enough and these rules were not fair and need to be changed."

I was in complete shock about what she did and what she said; I couldn't even say a word to her. She looked at me and said, "Rania, I will keep fighting for your rights. Do you have proof that what you wore to the park was a swimming suit that was made for water?"

"Yes!" I said. "If you search Islamic swimming suits online, many pictures of that swimming suit will come up," I added. "Great!! I need you to print me a paper from a web site as proof. Can you?" she said.

"Yes, I can, but why?" I asked her. "I will take this paper and attach a letter about what happened to you in that place, then I will send it to the mayor and to the congressman if I need to," she said firmly. "This place and his manger need to learn how to treat people nicely and fairly," she added.

My heart was beating so fast with everything she said. I was surprised with her reaction, happy to know that she loves me that much, and scared to death to do anything she said. What she said was more than what I could do or even think of. To go and argue with that man was a big step that my dad tried to stop me from doing. It was not easy to imagine what she was offering to do for me. She was so excited and ready to do what she said and, before she went home, she added, "Rania, try to print this paper today and bring it to me as fast as you can, and I will take care of everything else. I will wait for you!"

"OK," I said shyly. I was so embarrassed to tell her that I might not be able to do that. She took her steps back to the door when I stopped her and gave her a big hug. "Thank you so much for everything you did for me. I appreciate it so much and just today I knew that you are not just a friend or a neighbor, but you are a true sister to my heart."

"Rania, you are good people and that was not the way that you deserved to be treated," she said, left the house and left me with waves of thoughts and feelings. What should I do? How can I tell her that I am too afraid to take that step? How come she has all this energy and excitement to fight for me, and I don't have half of it to fight to myself? Later, I did go online, I did print the paper, but I remained silent. I couldn't give her that paper. She asked me many times about it. One day she mentioned that her husband told her that she shouldn't take that situation seriously because the person who had the problem is not taking it that way. And her husband was totally right.

I always say, when you see bad behavior from a Muslim, it's not because of his religion, but it is because of the bad societies that he grew up in. We didn't learn how to express ourselves; we don't learn how to defend ourselves; we don't learn how to seek our rights; we don't learn many important things for life. We learned at school that our prophet said, "Cleanliness is an important part of the Islamic faith," and in the same society I saw trash around me on the streets. I learned my prophet said, "A believer may commit sins but will never lie," and I have met many liars who act like they practice Islam. These were some examples from the society that I grew up in. Any society has the good and the bad. I have to mention also that I have learned many good things in the Egyptian society, but seeking my rights definitely was not one of them.

Now, and after years of living in the U.S., after I have met many different people, after I have learned many lessons, I am ready!! If this situation will happen again, I will fight for myself. I won't be afraid anymore. This situation is definitely one of the most important situations I have faced, not just because of what happened to me in the park, but also because of the amazing reaction that my great friend had for me. I will never forget every single second she spent thinking of me, fighting for me, calling and driving all the way for me. I will never forget the disappointment that I caused her because of my weakness. If I am lucky in this life, it is because I have known and met amazing American people like this lady, who are the true treasures and the most important part of the United States of America.

14   Why Ramadan?

Around 16 hours of a hot dry sunny summer day, these will be the hours of fasting every day for 30 days this summer. These are the days of the month "Ramadan." It is the ninth month of the Islamic lunar calendar, which has 12 months in all.

Fasting is the fourth pillar of Islam, and it means no food, no drinks (even water) and no sex, every day during Ramadan from sunrise to the sunset. Then, everything is allowed again from the sunset to the sunrise of the next day. The lunar calendar moves around the regular calendar, so Ramadan comes earlier by about 11 days a year. Ramadan starts again at the same time of the year every about 33 years.

I will put myself in your shoes for a minute. "Oh my!! These people are so weird and probably crazy. How will they enjoy their life or even survive, with no food or water a whole month in the summer?" Now it is my turn to put you in my shoes, and take you for a tour of a Muslim's brain and heart. I will tell you, why Ramadan. Why do Muslims from all over the world do something so difficult every

year? The majority of Muslims around the world are counting down to get to Ramadan. They pray every day to live until Ramadan. Here in my article I will try not to talk about Ramadan as a pillar of Islam. I'll explain it from a different point of view. It is my view that I have learned through life, and that has connected to that month.

Purifying the Soul

Most of religions believe that humans were created from clay (the Earth's mud) and that God gave them a soul from Him. Because of that, when we care for our *bodies*, we always use things that come from Earth (food or drinks) or get closer to other humans (who were made from Earth) or get closer to the earth itself (go to a farm, beach, or any place we like). When we want to take care of our *soul*, we think about praying to God, or remembering Him.

Any believer from any religion who has had that feeling of happiness and pleasure upon praying, heart and soul, after sincere prayer, will know what I am talking about. If you are a believer, you will know that life usually takes you away from remembering God. We have days when we don't really think of God until we face a hardship. That not only happens to you as believer, but it also happens to every believer because of life's distractions. In Ramadan, as a Muslim I try to put the Earth away, so I get to feel the soul more. During my fasting in Ramadan, when I am hungry or thirsty, my prayers have a different taste. I feel my soul more than on any regular day.

Feeling the poor

We all know that the world has billions of hungry poor people, people who have absolutely no food. They feel the hunger always, not just for one month, but for years. During my fasting on a hot, dry day in Ramadan was the best feeling I ever felt. When I went to help distribute meals for poor families, who may not have something to eat or a place to sleep. They were waiting with broken hearts for anyone who would offer them a meal. They took the meals with happiness. They were not worried anymore about what they would eat to break their fasting. I may forget about them for months and months, but I will never forget them when I share the hunger with them during my fasting in Ramadan.

Exercising Self-control

I always think of my life as a big intersection of roads, where God's orders are the traffic lights for me. So in every part of my life I have one thing I don't do (red), and the rest of things are green and yellow, so it is all my choice to decide either to go (on green) or be careful (on yellow). For example, in food, pork is red, what I think is bad for me is yellow, and anything else is green. The same rule I find in every part of life. Now when the light is red, and my eyes see there are no cars anywhere around me, and it is 100% safe for me to go, still I would not go, because I know that the safest thing is to wait for the green light. I don't want to get a ticket to pay either. I deal that way with my God in my life.

Now, there are so many different situations people may face that influence them to go on red. For example, bribing and stealing are "red" in Islam, but any Muslim may face the situation when he is in need of money and someone else is offering to bribe him.

Here he needs his maximum self-control. If that person is able to control himself from very important parts of his daily life (food-drinks-sex), which usually are green for him all year, then avoiding this kind of huge mistake or sin should be much easier for him.

This self-control doesn't mean that fasting during Ramadan prevents all mistakes and sins, but some Muslims may fast just because they are used to it, so they usually will not get the psychological benefits of fasting. That part explains how I feel when I go to lunch with my non-Muslim friends at work during Ramadan. They all are eating their lunches around me, and I am fasting. They feel bad for me because I smell the food and see them eating, but I feel the maximum strength of self-control and that makes me full of happiness, which is better than food sometimes.

Enjoying some health benefits

To talk about health benefits, the Egyptian traditions in Ramadan won't be an example. In Egypt, usually we don't consider the health benefits. This is because of how much food the Egyptians may cook and eat from sunset to sunrise. If we think well in Ramadan as I explained in 1, 2 and 3, we probably will think one more time about the amounts of food that we consume throughout Ramadan. Believe it or not, some Egyptians gain weight in Ramadan, because of that tradition. If we just eat a regular simple meal for Suhur (the meal before the sunrise), then a regular meal for Iftar (breakfast, breaking the fast), and just healthy snacks in between Iftar and Suhur, that will help us get all the health benefits of Ramadan. Eating more food does not keep the hunger away.

My body feels a little bit of hunger in the morning, an hour later a bit more, then I feel the maximum hunger for five to ten minutes. After that will not feel any hunger. That happens a couple times during the first days of Ramadan, but later my body gets used to eating when appropriate, so I don't suffer.

I usually explain my feelings in the second of Iftar (eating in the sunset) this way: food is like someone you love so much and you missed him for a while. When I am back with the food again after fasting, I feel that happiness.

During Ramadan, Muslims try to stop any bad habits they have during the year; things like smoking, swearing, not controlling their tempers. Also, they make amends with the family members and friends that they are having problems with before Ramadan. Sometimes, Ramadan is the only time when a family gets to eat together at the same time at each meal. They also try to gather with more family and friends every day in Ramadan. Not only does every family eat together, but most Muslims all around the world eat at the same time in their respective time zone.

Questions about Fasting

Do you feel dizzy or tired while fasting?

I personally never felt dizzy or tired during Ramadan, but I am sure some people may. That is usually during the first two or three days. Later, they usually feel fine. That is why it is always better that we practice fasting before Ramadan.

How do you get your energy for work and movement during the morning?

About the energy, after the first couple of days, the body systems all will change, so the body is not using the carbs and sugar from the blood directly, but the body uses the stored sugar in the liver. That is a great health benefit to the liver and for the whole body. So, that is why fasting never effects the energy. My dad used to drive my mom CRAZY in Ramadan; he usually gets his maximum energy during fasting, so he moves around the house like a bee, and plays so much soccer in the house. You can imagine what used to happen.

What about if you get sick?

When sick, traveling, (pregnancy, nursing, the monthly period, or soon after a women has been in labor) we don't fast. We may make these days up after Ramadan or pay money for each day to poor people, if we can't make up fasting.

**I hope you now understand some reasons of WHY RAMANDAN?

15   A Piece of the Puzzle

Hate? Really?

She was school teacher with a bright smile. I worked in that school a few years ago. She was always nice to me ever since I started to work there.

One day she asked me if I was forced to wear Hijab. I explained it was all my choice. Another day, she offered to read the Bible with me. I smiled and told her, "Thank you. I have read the Bible. I respect this book so much and agree with a lot of it."

Few months later she mentioned that she had read a book about a Saudi Arabian girl who had a really bad life in Saudi Arabia. Then she said, "That is a terrible country to live in."

I told her, "I have lived in Saudi Arabia for years. I disagree with things in the system there, but Saudi Arabia is a country like any other country. It has the good and the bad. The people there are nice and kind, and if one person had a bad experience and wrote a book about it, it doesn't mean they all are bad."

I also told her, "I knew people who have had terrible experiences in the U.S. They might have a chance to write a book about it. Some people may read it in another part of the world, and they may have the same bad idea about U.S. as the one you have now about Saudi Arabia. Just from one person's experience—don't you think that is not fair?"

She smiled and said, "Yes."

A Piece of the Puzzle

A couple months later, while about seven of us teachers were eating lunch, she looked at me and said, "Rania, did you read the Quran, your holy book?"

I said, "Sure I did, so many times."

She said, "My friend read about it, and he told me he found some verses in the Quran that order Muslims to kill anyone who is not Muslim."

I looked at her with shock, but I was trying to keep my smile. I said, "I read that book many times, as I said, and I read the explanation also. That is not true."

She said, "Anyway, my friend has those verses. I will bring them for you tomorrow."

I was not able to eat the rest of my lunch after her words; I needed to cry badly. I knew she wasn't trying to be mean to me. She is really nice and kind, but just to imagine the idea! It was hurtful that some people may think that, because I am a Muslim, I might kill them to practice my religion. Also, I thought about everyone else who was sitting with us around the lunch table. I trust my religion, and I would prove to her that was not true. But everyone else at the table who heard her words about the Quran might think that was true.

All of that was enough for me to go to the bathroom and burst out crying.

The next day she brought me a paper that had five verses from the Quran in English. She came to my classroom and gently she said, "Here are the verses that my friend found from the Quran."

I took the paper and said, "I will go home and read it, and I will get back to you."

A Piece of the Puzzle

I went home and, before doing anything else, I took the paper out of my purse. I sat on the couch while taking a deep breath, and I read it. I read the paper a couple times. The verses *do* say to kill the disbelievers. How come? I was raised in an Islamic country in a Muslim family. I always learned to respect others' beliefs, not to kill, not to lie, not to cheat, not to hate. I have read the Quran many times. I am the kind of person who doesn't like to read a book more than once, or watch a movie more than once. Despite that, I always love to read Quran because I always feel like a better person after I read it.

I decided to get an English Quran translation and see if these verses were really in the book. I opened it and found them all there. I was sure something was wrong, but I couldn't seem to find it. I was confused, so I decided to get the Quran in Arabic and in English and read these verses from both books to understand how this was possible.

When I did that, I actually read the chapters that have the verses. I read what verses are before and after them. Four of these five verses were from one chapter that had come for the Prophet at a very hard time, in a specific situation, during a period when Islam and Muslims were in a high danger. And the fifth verse was from another chapter. Now, I had better picture. I understood what happened.

I looked at the paper she gave to me. It was printed from a website on the Internet. I remembered her words to me. She had said her friend read ABOUT the Quran, *not* read the Quran itself. So the person who put them online took a part from the puzzle and put it online to give the reader a part of the picture that actually is the opposite of the real, whole picture.

I decided to read more about these verses from trusted Islamic books. I wanted to know the reasons for these verses and the stories behind them. The picture was clearer for me after I read. I decided to send the teacher an email with everything I had learned about these verses, so she would know that what she had said about killing non-Muslims was not true. I did write the email with my, then, poor English. I tried my best to explain everything as clearly as I could.

I went to bed that night in a great mood, because now it made sense. But I thought about the whole situation. How many non-Muslims in the world may have the same misunderstanding if they looked at that website? How many bad Muslims may brainwash young Muslims in the same way to make them into terrorists? The most important reason that there are Muslim terrorists from Islamic countries is that we don't have knowledge. And we also have bad education. Muslims who grow up in Islamic countries are mostly not good readers, even though the first word we believe that God sent in the Quran was "Read."

Right before I fell into a deep sleep in that night, I had a good idea! I woke up the next morning and went to my school. I went directly to this teacher's room.

I smiled and said, "Good morning!"

She said back, "Good morning."

I told her, "I sent you an email with everything about the verses." She said, "Thank you. I will read it when I go home."

I asked her, "Do you mind if I do a little experiment with you before you read my email?"

Surprised, she answered, "I don't mind! What experiment?"

A Piece of the Puzzle

I took a blank sheet of paper and a pen from her desk, then I wrote on the paper these words. (Let's say her name is Mary):

> Mary,
>
> I don't like you anymore. I love you !
>
> Rania

I looked at her and said, "What would you think if I wrote you this note and left it on your desk? Would you think I love you or hate you?" She said, "I would think that you love me very much!"

I took scissors from the top of her desk and cut the paper exactly in half. I told her, "Just imagine there is a person who hates me so much and came in the room before you saw this note. This individual cut the paper as I did now. Then he threw away half of it. You will come and read the note like this."

> Mary,
>
> I don't like you anymore.
>
> Rania

I said, "What would you think when you read this note?" She answered, "I would think you hate me."

I said, "But is this really what is in my heart for you?" She said, "No."

I told her, "That is exactly what happened with these verses that you gave me. If you hear bad things about any person, try to know that person first before you judge him. If you hear bad things about the Quran, read the Quran first as any other book you read, then judge it."

She smiled and said, "Thank you Rania. I will."

That was a really important situation in my life. I have learned a lot from this woman. I really love and respect her. And I am so happy she asked me and didn't keep her misunderstanding to herself forever. Hopefully, she told her friend about it also, so he would not keep spreading wrong information without even realizing how hurtful that might be.

Please always ask questions or read from trusted sources when you have questions about any group, any religion, or any person. If we always do that, we surely will make a huge difference in this world.

The Whole Puzzle

These are the five verses:

> Then, when the sacred months have passed, slay the idolaters wherever you find them, and take them (captive), and besiege them, and prepare for them each ambush. But if they repent and establish prayers and pay the poor-due (charity), then leave their way free. Lo! Allah is the most Forgiving, Merciful.
> *(Quran 9:5)*

> Fight against such of those who have been given the Scripture as believe not in Allah nor the Last Day, and forbid not that which Allah hath forbidden by His messenger, and follow not the Religion of Truth, until they pay the tribute readily, being brought low.
> *(Quran 9:29)*

> And the Jews say: Ezra is the son of Allah, and the Christians say: The Messiah is the son of Allah. That is

their saying with their mouths. They imitate the saying of those who disbelieved of old. Allah (Himself) fight against them. How perverse are they! *(Quran 9:30)*

O Prophet! Strive against the disbelievers and the hypocrites! Be harsh with them. Their ultimate abode is hell, a hapless journey's end. *(Quran 9:73)*

Those of the believers who sit still, other than those who have a (disabling) hurt, are not on an equality with those who strive in the way of Allah with their wealth and lives. Allah hath conferred on those who strive with their wealth and lives a rank above the sedentary. Unto each Allah hath promised good, but He hath bestowed on those who strive a great reward above the sedentary. *(Quran 4:95)*

I sent this email to her:

Dear friend,

Assalamu Alaikum (Peace be upon you). This is the Islamic greeting we should say it to everyone (like "hi" here) to have good deeds in Islam. You will find all Muslims in the Muslims countries say it to Muslims and to non-Muslims.

Before I start I want to tell you couple things,

-Arabic is a very rich and strong language and it's sometimes hard to translate the same exact Arabic meaning to any other language.

— We believe the Quran is God's words, and it is Prophet Muhammad's miracle. We believe that he is the only Prophet

who got a miracle which is seen to any believer any time until the end of the world and the Day of Judgment. The Quran was sent to him from God and Prophet Muhammad was illiterate. The Quran was revealed to him in perfect Arabic.

All the verses you gave to me are in the Quran, and it came during a hard time for the Muslims. You will find 4 of these verses from the same part, Chapter 9, which is Sūratu at-Tawbah, "The Repentance," and this surah came to Prophet Mohammed for a specific situation. Muslims were not allowed to fight; God ordered them not to fight at all, even to defend themselves for 13 years and before this chapter came. We have a verse that has the main rules for fighting. Any other verse that mentions fighting comes after this main rule:

> Fight against those who fight against you in the way of Allah, but do not transgress, for Allah does not love transgressors. (Quran 2:190)

During this time, there was a peace agreement between Muslims (as a small group of people then) and the unbelievers, who were controlling everything. Suddenly the unbelievers break the agreement to destroy Muslim and Islam. These verses came to encourage Muslims to defend themselves and their religion, and these verses were for the unbelievers in Makkah--just Makkah in that time during that situation, not everywhere else.

We can know that because every chapter and every verse in the Quran has a reason, and you can understand more if you read about Islamic history. That's what I did. I read so much about Islamic history and about verses' reasons, but the problem is that not everyone will do that. That's why some people get these verses from any website and may say many bad things about Muslims and the Quran. Unfortunately, some Muslims' bad actions give them the proof for it.

If you will have the chance to read the Quran, you will find so many verses in the Quran ask us to respect the other religions and to treat them good with all fairness and never hurt them.

I'll tell you the explanation to each verse you gave to me, and the reason behind it:

> Excepting those of the idolaters with whom you (Muslims) have an agreement, and who have since abated nothing of your right nor have supported anyone against you. (As for these), fulfill their agreement to them till their term. Lo! Allah love those who keep their duty. (*Quran 9:4*)

> Then, when the sacred months have passed, slay the idolaters wherever you find them, and take them (captive), and besiege them, and prepare for them each ambush. But if they repent and establish prayers and pay the poor-due (charity), then leave their way free. Lo! Allah is Forgiving, Merciful. (*Quran 9:5*)[1]

---

[1] This is one of the five verses on the paper Mary handed to me.

And if anyone of the idolaters seek the protection (O Muhammad), then protect him so that he may hear the Word of Allah, and afterward convey him to his place of safety. That is because they are a folk who know not. (*Quran 9:6*)

When you read the verses before and after verse 5 you will notice that the unbelievers are from Mecca, a holy city and the Prophet's homeland. When the unbelievers there were trying to kill and hurt all the Muslims in Makkah, even though God didn't ask the Muslim to kill all the unbelievers but he divided them to two kinds:

1- The unbelievers who are fighting you and trying to kill you in the battlefield (slay the idolaters wherever ye find them, or fight and slay the pagans as in your translation)

2- The unbelievers who are not fighting the Muslims directly but helping #1, take them captive and besiege them. etc, but if they stop trying to fight you directly or indirectly and started to have the peace between themselves and their creator (the prayers)-nobody can make sure of this one but God- and started to help their community (charity)-to the poor people not to Muslims- then forget everything they did and leave them free because Allah is forgiving and merciful and we have to be like this as Muslims. There is famous proof for what I'm saying in the Islamic history when the Prophet Mohammed (peace upon him) went back to Makkah after the unbelievers in Makkah forced him to leave with a small group of people who converted to Islam. They left Makkah secretly, because the unbelievers were beating them, torturing them, and killing them. Mohammed came back after 10 years with thousands of Muslims and entered

A Piece of the Puzzle

*Makkah (his home) again and the unbelievers were so afraid
of what he may do with all this huge amount of Muslims.
They thought he may take his revenge from them easily.
They asked him, "What will you do with us?" He said, "I'll
do nothing you can go. You are free." And they all stayed in
Makkah as unbelievers. Some of them converted to Islam
later and some didn't. They never got hurt, and it was all
peace in Makkah. I have one simpler thing to explain. We
have a Surah (Chapter 109) about the disbelievers. It has
the title ("The Disbelievers"). In Verses 1 through 6, it says*

> Say: O disbelievers!
> I do not worship what you worship;
> Nor are you worshippers of what I worship.
> Nort will I be a worshipper of what you worship.
> Nor will you be worshippers of what I worship.
> For you is *your* religion, and for me is *mine.*

*This means they have all the freedom to worship anything
they want. Most of the disbelievers were pagans back then,
but these verses were sent for any kind of disbelievers of
Islam.*

> Fight against such of those who have been given
> the Scripture as believe not in Allah nor the Last
> Day, and forbid not that which Allah hath
> forbidden by His messenger, and follow not the
> Religion of Truth, until they pay the tribute
> readily, being brought low. (Quran 9:29)[2]

---

[2] This is one of the five verses on the paper Mary handed to me.

A Piece of the Puzzle

The Muslims started to be a majority at Madina, which is the city they migrated to after being persecuted and harmed in Makkah. They had to assemble an army to protect themselves and everyone else in the city, even the non-Muslims.

They had just had years of fighting with the disbelievers; they were not sure how honest they might be as part of the army. The Muslims decided it's not a good idea to trust all the unbelievers to join their army, so, in this case, if somebody attacked the country just the Muslims will die. Then to be fair the unbelievers have to pay money to support the army which protects them, but the disbelievers refused to do so. Then came this verse and it does make since with the story. Because if they refuse to support the army, then they support the people who are attacking the Muslims.

The last part of it (being brought low) is because when you give money to somebody you may feel like you are doing a favor for him, but in this case they are being brought low because the Muslims are paying with their lives to protect them. The money is low when comparing it to life. Plus all Muslims paid charity as part of their religion and the Muslims give that charity to the poor people from Muslims and non-Muslims equally.

And the Jews say: Ezra is the son of Allah, and the Christians say: The Messiah is the son of Allah. That is their saying with their mouths. They imitate the saying of those who disbelieved of old. Allah (Himself) fight against them. How perverse are they! (*Quran 9:30*)[3]

In Islam, we believe in Jesus and Moses as great prophets just like Mohammed (Peace be upon them all). In Islam, Ezra was a great religious man, and he had his own story in the Quran. The meaning here is not the regular fight because God in Islam is not like us (nothing like Him) but the meaning here is they will be out of His mercy. Just as in the Christianity, those who doesn't believe in Jesus (peace upon him) as a son of God, will go to hell and God will not accept him in His mercy. And in any other religion you will find the same concept. Also another meaning for fighting here is to prove them that their thoughts are not true, so fight the ideas with different ideas. In the Quran, you find many other verses order us to not judge others, and describe the Christians with beautiful words. In this verse I always think of myself if many people decided that I have a child who I never had. How mad would I be? This verse is all about God not us as Muslims. In Islam we have a verse that says Allah is the only one who will judge anyone from any other religion not just Judaism and Christianity but even those who don't believe in God or who worship stars. And there is nothing in this verse you gave to me that encourages Muslims or asks them to fight the Jews or the Christians or anyone else!

Indeed, those who believed and those who were Jews or Christians or Sabeans - those [among them] who believed in Allah (God) and the Last Day and did righteousness - will have their

---

[3] This is one of the five verses on the paper Mary handed to me.

reward with their Lord, and no fear will there be
concerning them, nor will they grieve.
(*Quran 2:62*)

He is Allah, the One!
Allah, the Eternal Refuge
He neither begets nor is born
Nor is there to Him any equivalent.
(*Quran 112:1 - 4*)

O Prophet! Strive against the disbelievers and the
hypocrites! Be harsh with them. Their ultimate
abode is hell, a hapless journey's end.
(*Quran 9:73*)[4]

They swear by Allah that they did not say
[anything against the Prophet] while they had said
the word of disbelief and disbelieved after their
[pretense of] Islam and planned that which they
were not to attain. And they were not resentful
except [for the fact] that Allah and His Messenger
had enriched them of His bounty. So if they
repent, it is better for them; but if they turn
away, Allah will punish them with a painful
punishment in this world and the Hereafter. And
there will not be for them on earth any protector
or helper. (*Quran 9:74*)

When you read Verse 74 after 73, you will understand that
the order to strive against the disbelievers and the hypocrites
was for specific people during that time, and God gave the

---

[4] This is one of the five verses on the paper Mary handed to me.

A Piece of the Puzzle

signs of them in the next verse not to the unbelievers in general.

And remember all these are verses from just one chapter and we have 114 chapters. In hundreds of verses, Allah orders us to respect and love the unbelievers in general as

> Allah does not forbid you from those who do not fight you because of religion and do not expel you from your homes - from being righteous toward them and acting justly toward them. Indeed, Allah loves those who act justly. (*Quran 60:8*)

> O you who have believed, when you go forth [to fight] in the cause of Allah , investigate; and do not say to one who gives you [a greeting of] peace "You are not a believer," aspiring for the goods of worldly life; for with Allah are many acquisitions. You [yourselves] were like that before; then Allah conferred His favor upon you, so investigate. Indeed Allah is ever, with what you do, acquainted. (*Quran 4:94*)

> Those of the believers who sit still, other than those who have a (disabling) hurt, are not on an equality with those who strive in the way of Allah with their wealth and lives. Allah hath conferred on those who strive with their wealth and lives a rank above the sedentary. Unto each Allah hath promised good, but He hath bestowed on those

who strive a great reward above the sedentary;
(Quran 4:95)[5]

Degrees of rank from Him, and forgiveness and
mercy. Allah is ever Forgiving, Merciful.
(Quran 4:96)

*You will understand from the verse before 95 that the
meaning of the highlighted part is not to go to kill the
others at all. When the Muslims decided to let the cities
around them know about God (there were no books or media
1480 years ago to share with others about new things in the
world), they just wanted to speak with the people about this
new religion. Some of the leaders of these cities refused their
request to talk with people. The leaders were afraid that
they may lose their power from this new religion, so they
started to fight the Muslims.*

*Some of Muslims then were afraid to speak about their
religion because they may get hurt or get killed, but God
sent this verse to show the difference between the Muslims
who are brave enough to keep telling others about Islam and
those who were too afraid to do.*

*These verses are not for us now because there are so many
books and other resources available about Islam, and if
anyone wants to know about this religion from true sources,
they will know easily.*

*Just a reminder, these are five verses about a specific
situation from 6236 peaceful verses in the Quran.*

---

[5] This is one of the five verses on the paper Mary handed to me.

A Piece of the Puzzle

Thank you and I'm sorry if my email is too long. I did my best to give you the full idea because you mean a lot to me.

Let me know if you have any questions.

Love and respect,
Rania Zeithar

16   Understanding Islam and Me

What does the word "ISLAM" literally mean?

The word "Islam" means voluntary "submission" to God. It derives from the word "silm," which means "peace."

Islam is a natural way of life that encourages one to give due attention to his or her relationship with God and His creation. Islam teaches that it is through the doing of good deeds and seeking the pleasure of God and totally submitting to Him that souls find true happiness and peace in this world and the hereafter. It is in this context that the word Islam derives from the root word "silm" or peace.

What is the Islamic greeting?

It is "as-salaam-alaikum" (peace be upon you). The response is "wa-alaikum-as-salaam" (peace be upon you too).

Who are Muslims?

There are around 1.6 billion Muslims, which is almost one fourth of the world population. Estimates of Muslims in the United States of America range from 5 million to 8 million.

Muslims are people who believe in Islam. As believers, they worship one God and revere Prophet Muhammad, peace be upon him (PBUH), as the last messenger of God. Additionally, they also believe in all the prophets who preceded Prophet Muhammad (PBUH) and the holy books which they brought, such as the

Psalms, Torah, and the Gospel. A fundamental article of faith in Islam is believing in the Day of Judgment; also, Muslims believe in angels.

Prophet Muhammad said, "The real Muslim is a person who the people are safe from his tongue and his hands." (*Imam Ahmad and Al'Albani*)

Are all Muslims Arabs?

This is one of many misunderstandings about Muslims. Not all Muslims are Arab, not even most of Muslims are Arab. Just 15% of all Muslims around the world are Arab. Also, there are Arabs who are not Muslims (mostly Christians or Jews).

Muslims are everywhere all over the world. They speak the language of their home countries. Some non-Arab Muslims may learn Arabic to recite the Quran (The Muslims' holy book) in its original revelation language, Arabic.

The largest populations of Muslims are in Indonesia, then comes India. (*Source 9*)

What is the religion of Islam about?

It is an Abrahamic faith that teaches belief in one God.

It is a monotheistic faith that teaches belief in, worship of, and obedience to one God without partners or equals.

Muslims believe it is the same faith taught and practiced by all prophets throughout time, including Adam, Noah, Abraham, Moses, and Jesus (peace be upon them all). They also believe all prophets submitted to God alone, seeking peace in this world and the hereafter.

They believe all the creations are submitting to God naturally, and humans are given free will to choose to either accept God's message or not.

Who is Allah, the God of Muslims?

Muslims believe that they worship the same God as Jews and Christians. They believe He sent His message in different stages, and Islam was the last one.

The word "Allah" الله is the Arabic word for God; Arab Jews and Christians use the word "Allah" while referring to God in their holy books that are Arabic translations of Genesis and John.

What is the Quran?

Muslims consider the Quran the miracle of Allah and the final testament to humankind. They believe it is God's words to humanity. It was revealed in perfect Arabic to an illiterate man from God through the Angel Gabriel.

The word *quran* literally means "that which is often recited."

The Quran was memorized by Prophet Muhammad and his followers, dictated to his companions, and written down by scribes, who cross-checked it during the Prophet's lifetime. Prophet Muhammad (PBUH) memorized and reviewed the Quran many times with his companions before he passed away.

Most of the companions memorized the entire Quran, as did their followers. Then, it was collected into one book. Not one word of its 114 chapters has changed over the centuries. God promised in the Quran itself to protect this book from any changes until the end of the world.

The Quran is the principal source of every Muslim's faith and practice. It deals with all subjects that concern us as human beings, including wisdom, doctrine, worship, and law, but its basic theme is the relationship between God and His creation. At the same time, the Quran provides guidelines for a just society, proper human conduct, and equitable economic principles.

The meanings of the Quran are translated to almost every language on earth, but it is not considered Quran itself.

Facts about the Quran

"He [God] has sent down to you the Book [the Quran] with truth, confirming what was revealed before; And He sent down the Torah [of Moses] and the Gospel [of Jesus] before this as a guide in humankind; and He sent down the Criterion [the Quran]." *Quran 3:3-4*

Muslims read from the Quran day and night. They recite its opening chapter "Al-fatiha" at least 17 times in the five daily prayers. Muslims recite Quran on both celebratory and sad occasions.

The opening line of every Quranic chapter is "In the name of Allah, the most beneficent, the most merciful."

Quran is the only holy book that is memorized in its entirety in the world. It is four-fifths the size of the New Testament. Some Muslims commit all of its 86,430 words to memory. Those who do are called *hufaaz* (plural of *hafiz*, the one who remembers) and are held in high esteem. There are said to be 10 million of them. What makes the achievement of hufaaz more remarkable is that not all of them understand Arabic. In fact, the tradition of memorization is strongest in some non-Arabic nations, such as India.

The Quran consists of 114 chapters ranging in length from 3 to 286 verses. The entire text is divided into 30 parts, which were revealed intermittently in 23 years.

The word love is mentioned in the Quran 83 times. (I've included this fact because I've heard a rumor that the word "love" is never mentioned in the Muslim's holy book.)

The word "sword" has at least 65 synonyms in the Arabic language, and none of them is mentioned in the Quran once. (This fact is for another rumor that Islam was spread by sword.)

In the Quran, Moses is mentioned 135 times, Abraham 67, Noah 43, Jesus 33, Joseph 27, and Adam 25. Muhammad is mentioned by name 5 times. (Peace be upon them all.)

The only chapter named after a woman is titled "Mary," for the mother of Jesus (peace be upon them both).

The Quran has different kinds of verses:

- ○ Verses giving instructions to Muslims from God, to show them how to live and how to worship God.

- ○ Verses telling stories about prophets and other people before Prophet Muhammad (PBUH) to teach us lessons from their lives.

- ○ Verses about specific situations that happened during the Prophet Muhammad's (PBUH) time. These verses answered some questions they had or gave them solutions for some problems they had. Again, these verses are for us to learn from about their time.

- ○ Scientific verses which have scientific information which the world just discovered recently, such as origin of the universe, expansion of the universe, origin of life, nature of mountains, oceans, and lightning, and more.

    ◦   Verses describe God and the Hereafter.

The Quran refers to Jews and Christians by the noble title "People of the Book."

Dr. Jeffrey Lang, a professor of mathematics and a well-known convert to Islam has found that the Quran mentions the word "knowledge" or "reasoning" in various forms 854 times.

Who is Muhammad?

Muhammad (PBUH) is the prophet of Islam. Muslims believe he was the last in a line of prophets sent by God.

He was referred to as "the trustworthy" and "the truthful" among his people before he became a prophet.

He was orphaned at a young age. His dad passed away before he was born; then, his mom passed away when he was six years old. His grandfather took care of him until he also died. After that he was raised in his uncle's custody. Muhammad was illiterate, as were many people during this time.

He always shunned polytheism, the predominant religion of Arabia at the time.

He began receiving revelations from the Angel Gabriel when he was forty, the same age as Moses when he received his first revelation.

Revelations that made up the Muslims' holy book the *Quran* continued for twenty-three years until Prophet Muhammad passed away.

God said about Prophet Muhammad in the Quran, "And We have not sent you, [O Muhammad], except as a mercy to the worlds." *Quran 21:107*

Muhammad's (PBUH) Life
570 C.E. — Born in Makkah
- People of Arabia practiced polytheism

610 C.E. — Visited by Angel Gabriel on Mount Hira
- Revelation of the Quran teaching monotheism
- Early Muslims persecuted by Makkahns

622 C.E. — Migration of Muslims to Madinah
- Islamic calendar begins
- Establishment of Islamic state in Madinah

633 C.E. — Muhammad dies
- Islam spreads beyond Arabian Peninsula

The Wisdom of Muhammad

"The sayings of Muhammad are among the treasures of mankind." *Mahatma Gandhi*

- [on family] One who cuts off family ties does not enter Paradise.
- [on women] God enjoins you treat women well. Women are twin halves of men.
- [on the young] He is not one of us who does not treat the young with compassion.
- [on a neighbor] He is not a believer if his neighbor does not feel safe from him.

◆ [on moderation] Be moderate in religion.

◆ [on animals] Fear God in how you treat animals. (Treat them gently and remember you will be accountable before God for them)

◆ [on non-Muslims] All prophets are brothers, with different mothers but one religion.

◆ Don't consider me (Muhammad) better than Moses.

◆ Beware! Whoever is cruel and harsh to a non-Muslim minority, curtailing their rights, overburdening them, I will complain (to God) about that person on the Day of Judgment.

◆ Once Muhammad got up when a bier [conveyance of a coffin] went by, and he was told, "This is the bier of a Jew." He responded, "So what? Did it not have a soul?"

◆ I am (Muhammad) close to Jesus, in this world and the hereafter.

◆ As a Muslim, Muhammad (PBUH) left me a saying for every single part, action, situation, and movement in my life.

In my opinion

○ we don't need to be Christians to respect Christianity.

○ we don't need to be Jewish to respect Judaism.

○ we don't need to be Muslims to respect Islam and Prophet Muhammad (PBUH).

○ knowledge is the key to respect.

Non-Muslims' Views About Muhammad (PBUH)

This is a collection of short quotations from a wide variety of non-Muslim notables, including academics, writers, philosophers, poets, politicians, and activists belonging to the East and the West. None of them ever became a Muslim. These words, therefore, reflect their personal views on various aspects of the life of the Prophet Muhammed.

- ◆ **John William Draper** (May 5, 1811 – January 4, 1882) was an American (English-born) scientist, philosopher, physician, chemist, historian, and photographer. He is credited with producing the first clear photograph of a female face (1839 – 1840) and the first detailed photograph of the Moon (1840). He was also the first president of the American Chemical Society (1876 – 1877) and a founder of the New York University School of Medicine. He said "Four years after the death of Justinian, A.D. 569, was born at Makkah, in Arabia the man who, of all men exercised the greatest influence upon the human race. MUHAMMAD."

- ◆ **Michael H Hart** (Born on April 27, 1932) was an American astrophysicist, author, and a historian. His most famous book was *The 100: A ranking of the Most Influential Persons in History*. In his book he chose Prophet Muhammad to be the number one of the most influential persons in history. Hart recognized that ranking Muhammad first might be controversial, but felt that, from a secular historian's perspective, this was the correct choice because Muhammad is the only man to have been both a founder of a major world religion and a major military/political leader. He said

Muhammad was "supremely successful" in both the religious and secular realms.

♦ **Alphonse Marie Louis de Lamartine** (French 1790 – 1869) was a French writer, poet and politician who was instrumental in the foundation of the Second Republic and the continuation of the Tricolor as the flag of France. In his book, Histoire de la Turquie (1854), Alphonse de Lamartine writes, "If greatness of purpose, smallness of means, and astounding results are the three criteria of human genius, who could dare to compare any great man in modern history with Muhammad? The most famous men created arms, laws and empires only. They founded, if anything at all, no more than material powers, which often crumbled away before their eyes. This man moved not only armies, legislation, empires, peoples and dynasties, but millions of men in one-third of the then-inhabited world; and more than that he moved the altars, the gods, the religions, the ideas, the beliefs and souls."

♦ **Sarojini Naidu** was and Indian independence activist and poet. Naidu served as the first governor of the United Provinces of Agra and Oudh from 1947 to 1949, and the first woman to become the governor of an Indian state. She was the second woman to become the president of the Indian national congress in 1925 and the first Indian woman to do so. About Islam she said, "It was the first religion that preached and practiced democracy for, in the mosque, when the call for prayers is sounded and worshippers are gathered together, the democracy of Islam is embodied five times a day when the peasant and king kneel side by and side and proclaim, *God Alone is Great.* I have never been struck over and over again by this indivisible unity of Islam that makes man instinctively a brother."

♦ **Mahatma Gandhi's** statement published in Young India (1924) stated, "I wanted to know the best of the life of one who holds today an undisputed sway over the hearts of millions of mankind. I became more than ever convinced that it was not the sword that won a place for Islam in those days in the scheme of life. It was the rigid simplicity, the utter self-effacement of the Prophet, the scrupulous regard for pledges, his intense devotion to his friends and followers, his intrepidity, his fearlessness, his absolute trust in God and in his own mission. These and not the sword carried everything before them and surmounted every obstacle. When I closed the second volume (of the Prophet's biography), I was sorry there was not more for me to read of that great life."

♦ In 1935, The **United States Supreme Court** honored Muhammad, the Prophet of Islam, as a source of law and justice alongside Moses, Solomon, and Confucius. He is depicted in the Courtroom frieze among the great law-givers of mankind.

These were just some examples of great non-Muslims' opinions about a great man and his religion.

What are the pillars of the Islamic faith?

- One God without equals or partners
- Believing in His angels
- Believing in His revelations through the holy books.
- Believing in all of His prophets through the ages and centuries. There are many of them but the most prominent are Adam, Noah, Abraham, Ismail, Isaac, Jacob, Joseph, Moses, Jesus, (and Muhammad, as the last prophet (peace be upon them all).
- Believing in the Day of Judgment and the hereafter. Only God will judge all humans according to their deeds.
- Believing in destiny. The good and the bad, happen for reasons which only God knows. We have to be patient to understand it.

What are the pillars for practicing Islam?

- **The Testimony of Faith:** "There is no true god but God, and Muhammad is his messenger." It means that none has the right to be worshipped but God alone, and that God has neither partners nor equals. Muhammad is his last messenger and his servant. This testimony of faith is called the "shahada." The testimony of faith is the most important pillar of Islam.
- **Prayers:** Muslims perform five prayers a day. Each prayer does not take more than a few minutes to perform. Prayer in Islam is a direct link between the worshipper and God. Prayers are performed at dawn, noon, mid-afternoon, sunset, and night. A Muslim may

pray almost anywhere, such as in fields, offices, factories, or universities.

♦ **Zakat (charity):** The original meaning of the word "zakat" is both "purification" and "growth." Giving zakat means "giving a specific percentage on certain properties to certain classes of needy people." Zakat is 2.5% of the extra money a person saved for a whole year. A person may also give as much as he or she pleases as voluntary charity after the percentage of zakat.

♦ **Fasting the Month of Ramadan:** Every year in the month of Ramadan, which is the 9th month of the Islamic lunar calendar, all Muslims fast from dawn until sunset by abstaining from food, drink, and sexual relations. Although the fast is beneficial to health, it is regarded principally as a method of spiritual self-purification. By cutting oneself off from worldly comforts, even for a short time, a fasting person gains true sympathy with those who go hungry, as well as growth in his or her spiritual life.

♦ **The Pilgrimage to Makkah:** The annual pilgrimage "hajj" to Makkah is an obligation once in a lifetime for those who are physically and financially able to perform it. About two million people go to Makkah each year from every corner of the globe. Although Makkah is always filled with visitors, the annual hajj is performed in the twelfth month of the Islamic calendar. Pilgrims wear special simple clothes which strip away distinctions of class and culture, so that all stand equal before God.

Islam and Women

- *Women in Islam* is one of the most prominent misunderstandings about Islam in the West.
- There is 100% equality in all the rights and responsibilities between men and women in Islam.
- Many verses in the Quran and many of the Prophet Muhammad's sayings confirm this equality and make it clear.
- Islam is about knowledge and learning, which lead to logic. That is why the first word sent to Prophet Muhammad (PBUH) from the Quran was "Read."
- Details are presented in the Chapter titled "My Rights in Islam" on Page 157 of this book.

Islam and Violence

- Because of the literal meaning of this religion's name and the greeting of "peace be upon you" that God order Muslims to use in the Quran, it is clear that this religion is the opposite of violence.
- The violence that is happening in the name of Islam is actually political violence, and they are justifying themselves by stealing the name of the religion.
- There is no holy war in Islam. The word "jihad" means "any kind of struggle to achieve success in a good cause."

- Terrorism is not "jihad" at all, but a perversion of the holy text.
- The word "terrorism" has never been mentioned in Islamic history. It was only in the 1980s, when a group of extremists started fighting the Soviet Union in Afghanistan, that we heard the word "Islamic terrorism."
- Sixty American Muslims were victims on September 11, 2001. (*Source 4*)
- Al Qaeda killed seven times as many Muslims as non-Muslims. (*Source 5*)
- A U.N. report released recently found that ISIS had killed thousands of Muslims – both Sunni and Shia. And again they killed more Muslims than non-Muslims. (*Source 5*)
- According to reports from 2014, the CIA estimates that ISIS is made up of between 20,000 and 31,500 fighters. (*Source 6*)
- If we tally up the low and high estimates for all these groups, we can begin to have a sense of the total number of jihadist militants that are part of formal organizations around the globe. We found that on the low end, an estimated 85,000 men are fighting in jihadist groups around the world; on the high end, it is 106,000. (*Source 7*)
- If we consider the highest estimate, we will find out the 106,000 of 1.6 billion will make .0006%. That will be the total percentage of the non-peaceful Muslims in the

world and the rest 99.9994% are totally normal, peaceful people.

♦ The main reason that people don't see this truth about Muslims is the media.

What should you know as a non-Muslim about Muslims?

♦ Muslims are monotheists who respect all previous messages that they believe God sent before Islam.

♦ Lying, stealing, cheating, committing adultery, taking drugs, gambling, killing and any sin or bad deed are all forbidden in Islam and whoever is practicing Islam has to avoid all of them.

♦ They believe that Muhammad was sent as a mercy to creation. Muslims try to imitate him and follow his steps.

♦ Muslims eat everything but pork or anything derived from pigs.

♦ Muslims drink everything but alcohol. Since they believe the mind is the most important part to control human behavior, anything that may affect the mind's functions is forbidden in Islam.

♦ Most Muslims don't hug the opposite gender, and you may meet a Muslim who doesn't shake hands or touch the opposite gender. This is not so common.

♦ Muslims celebrate two big holidays which are equal to Christmas. Eid Al-Fitr is three days right after the fasting month of Ramadan, and Eid Al-Adha is four days right after the annual hajj pilgrimage to Makkah.

- Most Muslims don't celebrate Christmas, and those who do celebrate it for fun and not as a religious holiday. You may meet Muslims who celebrate other holidays such as Halloween and Easter while others prefer not to celebrate any holidays but the two Eids.

- Muslims believe in Jesus as one of the best five prophets who were sent to humanity. They believe in his miraculous birth, all his miracles, and his return before the end of the world. In the Quran, there are two more miracles about Jesus are not mentioned in the Bible.

- Muslims respect all prophets, and they believe that the prophets never committed any major sins in their lives.

- Muslims who practice Islam don't date or have a complete relationships with another partner before marriage.

- If you see a bad Muslim it is not because of his religion. It is because he is a bad person who doesn't practice his religion correctly.

- Respecting, understanding, and living peacefully with others are parts of practicing the religion of Islam.

- Please don't declaim that some association exists between the 0.0006% terrorists from the Muslims' population and the other 99.9994% of Muslims, who are peaceful. Terrorism hurts Muslims the most of all, because it's the opposite of their true religion.

Specific Facts About Islam and Muslims

- There are more Muslims in China than in Saudi Arabia.
- There are more Muslims in the UK than in Lebanon.
- 1.6 billion Muslims live, in total, on all inhabited continents of the world.
- There are tens of millions of Muslims in the U.S. & EU (European Union).
- One in every four people in the world is a Muslim.
- Islam is the world's second largest religion and the fastest growing. (*Source 8*)
- Nine Muslim astronauts have traveled to space.
- The world's first female space tourist was a Muslim woman.
- During the world's Dark Ages and Middle Ages, Muslims had the leading civilization. The most scientific inventions and discoveries, including algebra, anatomy of the eye, the first camera, hospitals, coffee, course meals, fashion trends, musical scales, and much more that changed the world came from the Muslim world. (*International award winning short video, starring Sir Ben Kingsley, Source 10*)
- When you search online about the most popular name in the world now, the name "Muhammad" will come up as the most popular, according to the Independent UK. This name is given to approximately 150 million men and boys all around the world.
- There's an estimated 15,000 Muslim soldiers (men and women) in the U.S. military, and 3,500 of them are

Arab American. (*American Muslim Armed Forces and Veterans Affairs Council and Source 3*)

♦ There are Muslim soldiers in most major Western armies.

♦ There are Muslim female police and military officers (and some wear a headscarf) in Sweden, Norway, UK, Canada, and U.S., among others.

♦ There are Muslim chaplains (Imams) in the U.S. army to serve Muslim soldiers and lead prayers and funerals.

♦ The majority of Muslims (over 1 billion adherents) are in Asia.

Sources

[1] http://www.islam101.com/history/population2_usa.html

[2] The book "Being Muslim" by Haroon Sidiqqui

[3] http://www.voanews.com/content/a-13-2007-02-15-voa46-66704312/559426.html

[4] http://islam.about.com/cs/currentevents/a/9_11statements.htm

[5] http://www.cnn.com/2015/01/15/opinion/obeidallah-al-qaeda-hypocrisy/

[6] http://thehill.com/policy/217514-cia-isis-made-of-20000-to-31500-fighters-

[7] http://www.cnn.com/2014/09/26/opinion/bergen-schneider-how-many-jihadists

[8] http://www.cnn.com/2015/04/02/living/pew-study-religion/

[9] http://www.pewforum.org/2015/04/02/muslims/pf_15-04-02_projectionstables74/

[10] http://www.1001inventions.com/media/video/library

17   Don't Blow It Up!

fiction by Rania Zeithar

"Good morning, my love," said Linda.

He opened his little eyes on his comfortable and cozy bed, looked at his mom's face, smiled, and said, "Good morning, Mom."

His mom played with his soft brown hair as she asked, "Did you sleep well, my sweetheart?"

"No, not really mom. I was so excited for our day. I was thinking of all of the things that we will do, and when I slept, I actually dreamed about all these things," he said.

"I thought you would go in a deep sleep after our long day shopping yesterday. You were very tired, weren't you?" she wondered.

"Yes, Mom, but how I could stop my brain thinking that I will see my family for the first time? Just in a few hours, I will hug my grandparents for real," he said as he was sitting up on his bed with so much happiness and excitement in his beautiful green eyes.

"Yes! For real, my little muffin! Now, you need to get up and be ready for our best day ever to see our big family," said Linda, with a louder voice and a big smile.

Linda didn't tell her son that she couldn't sleep for a minute the entire night. She also couldn't believe that she finally will go to back home to France. And finally she will see her beloved family after six years of suffering and separation.

Today was the first time happiness visited her heart since she lost her husband in a car accident one year ago. Sammy was her friend, her true love, the father of her only son, and her supporter in life. Losing him felt like she lost the main thing in her life, and she started to lose herself after him. But Adam, her eight year old boy, brought her life back. She still had a living part of her husband in Adam. He looks exactly like his dad, he is wise like his dad, he enjoys the food she cooks just like his dad. He shows the same kindness, caring, and even when he is angry at her, he sounds exactly like his dad.

"Come on, Adam. Breakfast is ready!"

"Yes, Mom. I am coming!" Adam answered, remembering an old day.

Adam! Get out of my chair now! said Sammy.

Why dad? Why do you always like to sit here? said Adam.

I love to always sit in this chair so I can see you and your beautiful mom in front of my eyes while eating every meal, Sammy said.

Linda and Adam sat at the small dining table in the kitchen, where they always like to eat. They always had the third chair at the table with Sammy's coat on it. They had decided not to touch it, except to wash the coat and put it back. It gave them the feeling that he always there with them.

"We have five hours to get everything ready for the trip, Adam. The cab will be here at 1:00 pm to give us the ride to JFK," Linda said while eating pancakes.

"Don't worry, Mom. I will get all my things ready in just two hours and will spend the rest of the time thinking what I will do with my grandparents, my aunt, and my uncles. I know you have one sister, Mom, but how many brothers did my dad have?" asked Adam, before drinking some milk from his cup.

"Your dad had four brothers, but I don't think we will see all of them on this trip," said Linda.

"Why mom?" asked Adam.

"Not all of them live in France now. Just two of them live in France; one around Paris and the other in Aries in south France. The other two moved out of France many years ago, after the death of their parents," said Linda.

"My friends are jealous of me because I will go to France, and I will be out of school for three weeks. I don't know why you didn't wait to go there in the summer as you told me before, but I really don't care. I just want to go there," said Adam, chewing his food.

"I told you, Adam, the plane tickets are much cheaper now than the summer," said Linda, while avoiding Adam's eyes.

"Does my family in France speak English, Mom? They always say very little on the phone in their French accent. Hi, how are you? And I miss you," said Adam in his best impression of his grandparents' English. "I am afraid this is all the English they know. I have many stories to tell them and questions to ask them, Mom," continued Adam in a soft voice.

Linda grinned, then added, "Your grandparents know a little bit of English, but your Aunt Nancy can talk much better English. Don't worry about that, my muffin. I promise you will get to do everything you want in this trip. Now, let's stop talking, and finish our breakfast fast to get ourselves ready."

She didn't tell him that they have to travel *now* to see his grandfather because he is sick, and Linda couldn't wait any more to see her dad and give him a hug, which might be the last one. Linda's dad had a couple of heart attacks before, but this last one was the worst. He just came out of the hospital, but he was not allowed to move from his bed. For the past ten years of his life, he was not allowed to exert himself or travel by plane after the serious heart surgery he had in 2005. That's why he couldn't come to visit them in the U.S. all these years. Also, her mom was diagnosed with multiple sclerosis, which made her lose the ability to walk eight years ago. Recently, she started to lose functions also. All of her parents' health problems put so much pressure on Linda when she was not able to leave the U.S. to see her beloved ones or hug them. She was always so worried to lose either of them before she could see them again.

The five hours went by fast, and soon the cab was ready to take Linda and Adam to JFK airport. They didn't pack enough clothes to stay there for three weeks, but Linda promised Adam he could buy more clothes in the "City of Lights." They checked in, and during their way to the gate, Linda's thoughts went back six years ago to remember everything that had happened before her first steps on the airplane to come to the U.S.

Linda was born in Saint-Denis, a northern suburb of Paris. Her parents were very caring and loving to her, and to her only sister Nancy, who was born two years after her. Linda finished her bachelor's degree, master's and PhD in psychology from Paris-Sorbonne University. She met her first love when she took her car to be fixed. Sammy was a handsome, smart, and kind man who was working as a mechanic in Paris. His family had emigrated from Morocco to France a long time before. He was the third generation in France. He didn't have or he didn't know of any family members who were still in Morocco. She loved how he took care of his whole family financially after the death of his dad when he was in high school. She loved how he loved traveling and discovering the world, especially to his country of origin, Morocco. Most of all, she loved how quickly he fell in love with her.

Linda's family was not very happy with her choice to marry Sammy. They always thought she deserved better than a mechanic. They didn't see in Sammy all the amazing things that Linda saw in him. Even after Linda and Sammy had their son, the relationship between her family and her husband was very cold. Sammy tried hard, but after a while he lost hope, and she never blamed him.

She remembered very well the day after her son turned two, when she got the offer letter to become a professor at Cornell University in New York. Cornell was one of the ten best universities in the USA and one of the 19 best in the world. A dream that she had had for years came true for her. Sammy never minded doing anything that would make her happy and successful. Deciding to leave her family and her beloved country was not easy for her or for them. But she promised her family that she would come to visit them at least once a year, so they would get to see how their only grandchild was growing.

She always had a great sense of self-esteem. She was on her way to the States, and she was sure that by being accepted to teach in one of their universities, they would actually be the ones to gain. She had always been one of the best students. Learning, reading, and understanding and observing were keys for her success as a student, as professor, and as a successful psychologist.

Don't Blow It Up!

It took a while for Linda and Sammy to pass the immigration line in the airport because of some checking, which took longer than it should. They entered the U.S. for the first time, and they were full of hope for a great new life. But this great new life didn't last more than a year.

In the first year, everything was just perfect. Linda established herself in her new job, Sammy found a job quickly, and Adam started to attend a day care facility. Everything was going in the right direction until the day that they decided to become American citizens. They thought it would be really good for them if they could have dual citizenship, French and American. They just needed to start their paper work and apply for the citizenship. They did, but what happened to them was not expected at all. Two months after they filed the paper work, they woke up one morning to loud knocking on their apartment door.

Sammy ran to the door, and Linda followed him. He opened the door to see two men. They knew from the first second these two men were law officers. One of the two men showed his badge and asked, "Are you Sammy Saied?"

He answered with a nervous voice, "Yes, I am Sammy. May I help you?"

"You need to come with us now to answer some questions at the FBI office. Please get yourself ready, and we will wait for you here to join us," one of the officers said firmly.

Sammy and Linda were in complete shock. Why were these officers here? Why would they want to take Sammy with them? What happened?

Linda looked at her husband's face with all these questions in her eyes and asked him, "Sammy, do you have any answers?"

Sammy looked at her and said with so much confusion, "I don't know anything. I have no idea what is happening, Linda!"

"Can I come with you, Sammy? I will go out and ask them if I can," she said, moving to the door.

"No, Linda, wait here. We don't have any place to leave Adam right now. I think it's just a mistake, or maybe they need to ask me about someone else. Don't worry. I will call to tell you what happened and hopefully will come back soon," Sammy said on his way out with the officers.

"Mom, are we there yet? I think I slept for too long," said Adam, to get his mom back from her emotional thoughts.

"You just slept for two hours, Adam. We need almost seven more hours to arrive in Paris. Relax and try to sleep some more, my muffin," Linda said, giving Adam a hug from the side. She put his head on her to help him go back sleep or maybe to help herself feel more secure. Security is what she really missed in the past few years of her life.

Just a couple of minutes were enough for Adam to go back into a deep sleep, then he left her again to swim in the dark sea of thoughts and memories all by herself.

She didn't remember exactly how many hours Sammy spent in the FBI office on that day, but she remember how hard, long, stressful and scary those hours were for her. He didn't come back for a long time, he didn't call as he promised, and she had no idea what to do or whom to call.

Her phone rang while she was thinking, and finally she saw her husband's name on it. She answered quickly and said "Sammy, are you OK? Where are you? Why are you not here yet?" A couple seconds passed, then Sammy said, "Linda, I need a lawyer. Try to get me one as soon as possible."

Linda couldn't control her tears when she heard him, and she said, "Sammy, what is happening? Why do you need a lawyer?"

"Linda, please calm down. I don't know everything yet. All I know is that my first name and my last name match another person's name who is on the terrorists list," Sammy said, with a nervous voice.

"What?! No way, you are the last person on earth who would have to do anything with these monsters," she said bursting into tears.

"Linda, please! What I need now is all your strength to help me prove to them that I am innocent. Please call a lawyer as soon as you can, and I will call you again to tell you what to do." he said and hung up the phone.

After this phone call they went through a very hard period of their life. It was not easy to prove that he was not the same person who was the terrorist, since the terrorist was in Morocco around the same period of time that Sammy had a vacation there.

They spent five years in investigations, accusations, courts, under pressure, and their paper work being held up until finally the FBI with the help of Interpol were able to find the real terrorist who had the same name. During these years, Sammy suffered depression as a result of the change of attitudes of everyone around him. He lost his job, and he lost his new friends, who were suspicious of him. Linda couldn't leave him a second; she was always by him, trying to give him all the strength and the support he needed. Just ten months after the happiness of his finally being proven innocent, he lost his life, and they lost him forever in the accident.

"We are landing. Please remain seated," the pilot announced. Linda found that she was crying, and her tears were falling on her son's face. She wiped her tears quickly, hoping that her son wouldn't wake up and see her crying, and she hoped that no one around would notice her quiet tears. She took a deep breath and looked out the airplane's window to the beautiful view of the clouds hugging each other and hanging in the sky.

"Mom, are we in Paris now?" asked Adam with his tired voice, as his eyes were looking around with excitement.

"Yes, we are! Now we need to find your Auntie; she is here somewhere waiting for us," said Linda while carrying her purse and their hand bag and walking to the arrival hall.

Nancy looked like she gained weight; she was not that skinny girl anymore, but she still had the same beautiful, bright smile. When Linda saw her sister, she wasn't sure if she was laughing or crying; she was feeling waves of happiness mixed with the pain of her suffering and longing.

Every step she took in her beloved city, on the way to her family's home, was bringing her a memory and a smile of her old happy days in France.

Loud laughs, stories, hugs and joy were in the house after she saw her mom and dad. They looked different. They seemed much older. It was as if she hadn't seen them for twenty years rather than six, but she was happy that she finally saw them and touched them with her hand and spent the best moments in their embraces. She spent the best week of her life with them. They didn't talk about any sad memories, and they didn't ask any questions about her hard six years. She really appreciated that; she tried her best to enjoy her time with them, and to help her son to enjoy his big family for the first time, until one day.

"Mom, I really want to see that place which you always told me about," said Adam

"Which place, Adam?" wondered Linda.

"The beautiful, very old building that my grandpa used to take you to watch movies and listen to bands from all over the world," said Adam.

"I think you mean the Bataclan theatre. We certainly will go there on our vacation. It is my favorite place in Paris, and my first date with your dad was there. Look! I was thinking where should we go in two days for my birthday? What do you think if we go there?" asked Linda with a smile.

"Yes, Mom, please! But I really want all my family to come with us there," said Adam.

"Sounds like a plan! I will tell your grandparents, your aunt, and your uncles, too. Even though it will not be easy for your grandparents to go anywhere because of their health problems, but good thing the doctor just allowed your grandpa to move. I am sure they will do anything they can, just for you, my muffin," said Linda. She felt all the happiness to see this big smile on her child's beautiful face.

The Bataclan, a beautiful old building which was designed in 1864, has been one of the most famous entertaining places in France. It has a café, music hall, and a theatre. The whole family decided to go there together to celebrate Linda's birthday, and then Linda would go with her sister to enjoy their favorite

American rock band, which was performing at the Bataclan that night.

"Should we take them home first, then come back for the concert?" Linda asked her sister.

"They will be fine. I know they all are taking a walk in the building now, and I trust that your brother-in-law Jim will stay with them until they are home. He looked very handsome today, by the way, and I should see him more often," said Nancy with a smile. Then she added, holding her sister's hand tight, "Don't worry, and let's enjoy your birthday night."

"I will call them now just to make sure everything is OK," said Linda. She looked on her phone to find three missed calls from her dad.

"Dad, are you OK?" asked Linda in French.

"We are fine, sweetie. We just forgot the house key with Nancy. I will send you Adam, with special permission from the ticket agent to get the key from her, and we will wait for him here in the cafeteria. He wanted to get a good night kiss from you before he goes home," said her dad.

"Okay, Dad. I will wait for him by the main door to bring you the key," said Linda smiling. She kept looking around in the crowds until she saw her little boy coming towards her. "Come on, Adam. I will take you to get the key from Nancy, and I will bring you back here," said Linda.

They were walking together in the loud big concert hall holding hands when all of a sudden they heard gun shots and loud screams. Linda hugged Adam quickly and leaned by the side wall.

"Mom, what is happening? I am so scared!" asked Adam in a panic.

"I don't know, Adam! Calm down, and we will try to get out of here as soon as we can," said Linda.

At the same second, she saw a very tall man holding a gun running their way to block the main door. She heard him talking in the Bluetooth headphone.

"I tried to get it, but I couldn't. It slipped in a small crack by the wall. I don't know what to do. I have to get it as fast as I can." Silence for a couple of seconds then he continued, "Yes, a child is a good idea!"

He was shooting while talking. He seemed to not see the horrified faces that were watching the blood everywhere, or to even hear the begging screams around him. He seemed to be in a totally different place, very calm and well organized. He was looking around until he saw Adam sitting with his mom by the wall, crying. He pointed to him with the gun and said, "You, little boy, come here now and get me this remote." He pointed to a small crack in the old floor.

"I need this *now*, or I will kill you," he continued.

"No, Adam, don't go! He wants you to get a remote to bomb the place. Don't do it!" said Linda while crying.

The tall man ran fast at them, grabbed Linda by her hair and pointed at her head with his gun, while another armed man was securing his back.

"You will stand up right now. Get me the remote or I will kill your mom in front of your eyes before I will kill you," said the tall man.

"No, please don't kill her! I will do whatever you want. I will get it for you," said Adam, choking on tears. Then Linda looked at Adam with a look that he clearly understood.

Don't Blow It Up!

"Why? Why all this blood?" asked Linda to the man who was strangling her. She was gathering up all her self-control and all the psychology she had learned all her life, in an attempt to stretch time until the police came.

"It's a war! They are trying to destroy us Muslims everywhere in the world. Don't you see! They bomb and kill civilian Muslims in Iraq, Afghanistan, Libya, Palestine, Syria and more? The list can keep going! The West kills us and our families every day and takes our lands. Don't you think it's a war yet?" He put more pressure on her neck with his strong arm.

"Okay! I understand what you say, but do you think what you do now will save Muslims, or will it be a good reason for the West to kill more Muslims?" she asked, despite the pressure on her neck.

"I follow my leader. He knows better, and I trust him," said the tall man firmly.

"What about Muhammed?" she asked.

"Who is Muhammad?" he asked.

"Your Prophet," said Linda.

"My Prophet had wars with enemies and he killed them," said the man.

"Yes, you just said wars! It was always between two armies in a specific place and specific time. Your Prophet was the only war leader in history that asked his soldiers not to cut a tree, not to kill a woman or a child or an elder, and not to destroy a place of worship during wars. Do you think you are still following him by killing all these innocent people now?" she asked.

"Don't say innocent! They are not; they chose their leaders who killed my own innocent family in the front of my eyes with their air strikes. They don't care about our lives. Why should I care about theirs? They just want to kill more Muslims and destroy Islam," he said angrily.

"And you are not?" she asked softly trying to avoid his irritation.

"No, I am defending Muslims and Islam and taking their revenge," he said.

"I am a Muslim. You will kill me and all my family, and you will make all the Muslims' lives out there hard as a hell," she said.

"No, you are not!" He screamed and got his gun ready to shoot.

She grabbed her necklace up and held it up to his face. It was inscribed with the words "There is no god but one God and Muhammad is His messenger."

He seemed very confused and looked at the little boy who was trying to get at the remote and made it fall back in the crack on purpose hoping to waste some time; he understood from his mom's look and was hoping for help to come soon.

"I can get you and your son out of here now," he said looking around.

"I will never go and leave all these people to die. I believe in the Quran, which says, *Whoever kills a person unjustly, it is as though he has killed all mankind. And whoever saves a life, it is as though he had saved all mankind.* God said *a person,* no matter what his religion or race. If you believe in the same religion I believe, get *everyone* out of here right now! Please, don't blow it up!" she said firmly as a last try.

The other armed man noticed that it was taking too long. He got the remote quickly from Adam's hand and pressed it. At the same instant, Linda and the tall man saw what was happening, and the man said with a nervous voice and tears filling his eyes, "Now, it's too late."

Don't Blow It Up!

After one second all of their blood was mixed around on the same place, with pain in the whole world.

18 Je Suis Rania

My dad! He is my role model. He means the world to me. He taught me so much in life. He helped me to know who I am, how to seek knowledge, and he fostered in my heart the love of learning. He always encouraged me to think, and to find reasons for everything I do. He taught me to respect others, and always think positively of them; even if they did something bad, always allow them excuses, and forgive them. I love my dad, not just because he is my dad, but because of everything he did to help me become who I am now, and to improve myself every day.

Just imagine for a moment that I went to my school one day to find that a bully drew a picture of my dad; he pictured him as an evil man. He also wrote my dad's name on the picture, mentioned my name, then hung it on the main wall in the school, so everyone could see it prominently displayed. What do you think my feelings were when I saw that with my own eyes?

Now you need to know that I as a Muslim love prophet Muhammad (peace be upon him) more than I love my dad, as the majority of Muslims do, not just because he is my prophet, but because he has done for me everything I mentioned about my dad and even more. It is hurtful for any Muslim to see or to know that a person has made fun of our beloved prophet. There are around 1.6 billion Muslims on earth who were hurt by that, even the Muslims who are not really practicing Islam.

Let's go back to my imaginary picture. If that bully hadn't drawn my own dad's picture and put it on the school wall, but instead he actually drew my friend's dad, how do you think I would feel? I would feel the same intense pain, especially if I knew how awesome my friend's dad was. I am always distressed when the media makes fun of the Pope or nuns or rabbis or any representation symbol of any other religion. I respect them all, and I never thought of making fun of them as being "freedom of speech."

We teach our students here in the American school to respect others, not to make fun of any religion or a race. But other people will teach them to do the opposite when they grow up, citing freedom of speech!! I understand the freedom to talk about your own society, the freedom to talk about your own politicians, or your own life, but to talk about other people's religions with mockery and distortion is not exercising freedom, but disrespect.

It was a surprise for me to know that the same magazine *Charlie Hebdo*, which published a mockery of cartoons about Prophet Mohamed (PBUH) as a form of freedom of speech, fired a French cartoonist who was working for them in 2009. His name was Sine. He wasn't just fired, but also he was charged with anti-Semitism for accusing Jean Sarkozy, the son of the French president, of converting to Judaism for financial reasons. Now Sine was not making fun of a Jewish Prophet or even an important rabbi, he just made fun of a normal person that he thought he was bad. He was fired and charged in a crime! Where is the freedom of speech now? If you are supporting *Charlie Hebdo* and joined "Je suis Charlie" because of the freedom of speech, be fair and think about that one more time.

Je Suis Rania

As a Muslim I totally disagreed with what the Charlie Hebdo newspaper did from the beginning, but I never talked about it. They were not the first people to do so; other people and other newspapers did the same thing a couple of years ago. It hurt, but when I heard about it, I thought right away of my prophet Muhammad. What would he do if he witnessed that?

He actually had so many of the same situations in his own life, since he knew he was a prophet and many people in Makkah hated that. They did everything you can imagine to stop him from spreading God's message. He always was patient and never responded. They said bad words about him, they said he was crazy, they said he was a magician, they threw garbage and trash on him. He never responded, except with good words and prayers.

Even the Quran, which we believe has an answer for every question, told us directly what to do if we heard people making fun of God (Allah) or his messenger.

> And it has already come down to you in the book that
> when you hear the verses of Allah [recited], they are
> denied [by them] and ridiculed; so don't sit with
> them until they enter into another conversation...
> (Quran 4:140)

So when people make fun of or mock God, His book or His messenger, God didn't order us to get mad, fight or scream or hate. He didn't even ask us to ignore them forever. He said don't be with them or talk with them until they change the subject, then you can talk again with them. Also, we have many other verses that ask us to be patient with any hater and only respond with good words and good actions.

In the prophet's life, many other situations he faced may help us to understand how we should act. He had a non-Muslim neighbor who hated him the most and used to put trash in the front of his house every morning. He never got mad at her or tried to kill her. He ignored her action until one day, when she didn't put trash, he asked about her and knew she was sick. Do you know what he did? He went to her house to visit her and to offer her help. Another example: Omar ebn elkhatab hated the prophet so much and decided to kill him. The prophet knew his hatred. The only thing he did was to pray for him.

Omar went to the Prophet's house to kill him. Neither the Prophet nor any of the believers tried to defend the prophet by killing Omar or even attacking him. He went to the house and heard the prophet reciting the Quran. After a while he changed from a hater to a Muslim who led the whole Muslim nation years after the Prophet's death. And he was one of the best and one of the fairest Muslim leaders in history. Remember "Love will not bring but love." Pray for the haters, at least to have enough knowledge that might make them understand other people. Pray for them to have peace in their hearts, so they may spread it.

The terrorists who attacked the building of *Charlie Hebdo* in France don't belong to me or to my religion in any way. My religion is under attack from two sides: one is informed non-Muslims filled with hate, the other is Muslims in name only who follow blindly, support violence, and increase the hate. In between them are hundreds of millions of peaceful Muslims who know what the real Islam is, but suffer from the actions and words of the two other sides.

If any non-Muslim hates ISIS or any terrorism in the name of Islam, any true Muslim hates them four times more, because they kill innocent people, because they kill them by stealing the name of Islam, because they do the opposite of what his God and his messenger commanded. And finally, that peaceful Muslim suffers in his life because of something he didn't do, doesn't like and doesn't support.

My religion is pure and innocent of the attacks and none of the Muslims I know supported that or were happy of what ISIS did. Terrorism is far from the meanings and teachings of my religion, even the farthest from the literal meaning of the word *Islam*, which is to submit PEACEFULLY to God. If you are not submitting to God, or not peacefully, then you are not a Muslim, even if you call yourself a Muslim. You don't belong to me or to my religion.

19 My Rights in Islam

I am a Muslim woman who was raised in a Muslim family who practiced Islam in a Muslim country. I have never felt for a second that I am oppressed as a woman. I have never felt that I am less than any man. I have never seen my dad treat my mom any less as a human. My parents have never put my brothers in a position over me. I always feel that my religion treats me like a princess, and that my Hijab, which I choose to wear, is just my crown. What I am explaining now isn't just about me, but millions of other Muslim women who are like me. Also, one more point to consider here: the majority of converts to Islam are women, and I don't think they would choose, with their own will, a religion that would oppress them.

When I came to the United States and watched the media, I was surprised that they always show Muslim women as poor, oppressed women who never have rights. They show a very small percentage of Muslim women that I rarely met or heard about in Egypt.

I have to make it clear that I don't say there is no oppression against women in Egypt or any other Muslim countries, but what I say is that this oppression comes from those who don't practice the religion of Islam or who are practicing it the totally wrong way.

In Islam, men and women are meant to complete each other, not to compete with each other. Here I will try to cover most of the discussions and questions about women in Islam.

Women in Pre-Islamic Society

Women suffered great injustices in pagan Arab society. They faced all kinds of humiliation before the mission of Muhammad as Messenger of God (peace be upon him). They were treated like material property to be disposed of at the whim of a male guardian. They had no rights at all. They were not allowed to inherit from their parents or husbands.

As a general practice, men had the freedom to have as many wives as they desired with no set limits. There was no system of law and justice that forbade a man from committing any injustice toward his wives. Women had no right to choose or even to refuse being chosen as a partner for marriage; they were simply given away. Women were forbidden to remarry if a husband divorced them, and they could be sold as goods in markets.

In the pre-Islamic era of Arabia, fathers commonly became extremely angry, disgraced, and sad with the birth of a female child into their family. The hatred of female babies prompted Arabs to bury them alive. That was really common back then. Women were not even able to practice some of the most natural of rights, such as eating certain types of foods that could only be eaten by men. Many males who later became Muslims used to do all these barbaric behaviors as a daily normal part of their lives.

This treatment of women in the Arab society led Umar ibn al-Khattab, the second caliph of the Muslims to say:

> By Allah, we didn't use to think that women had anything until Allah revealed about them what He revealed in the Qur'an, and distributed to them what He distributed…" (Bukhari 4621 and Muslim 31)

Many similar practices against women were in other cultures around the world during that time before 570 C.E.

Women's Rights in Islam

The issue of women in Islam is a topic of great misunderstanding and distortion due partly to a lack of knowledge, but also partly because of the misbehavior of some Muslims that has been taken to represent the teachings of Islam itself. These misbehaviors are totally from the men's culture, not from the religion of Islam. I will speak here about what Islam teaches, and that is the standard by which Muslims should be judged. The main sources for the religion of Islam are the Quran (the words of Allah) and the sayings of the Prophet (PBUH), his deeds, and his confirmation (Sunnah). These two sources are the basis for Islamic law (Shariah).

Here before talking about women in Islam, I need to clarify the word Shariah, which seems scary for some American people because of the media's misconception, but is it really scary? Muslims believe the Shariah is the set of laws and rules which God sent for them to follow in order to be good humans and build good societies. Shariah covers every single part of a Muslim's life, and we can discuss it in three main categories:

- ○ Beliefs (one God, his Prophets, books, angels, and the hereafter, etc.)

- ○ Character (What I should do to be a good human being, humility, kindness, smiling, patience, etc.; and what I should avoid, such as pride, lying, stealing, killing, cheating)

○ Actions (related to God, such as praying, fasting, charity; and actions related to other humans, such as marriage, business, crimes.)

In order to understand the punishment law in Shariah we have to know the Quran is 6,236 verses, only 80 of them about specific legal injunctions and fewer about the punishments, which total less than 1% of the Quran. So when I see the media presenting this 1% as 100%, without explaining this Islamic punishment system well, I consider them to be creating a major misconception about my religion.

The following sections discuss the position of women from a spiritual, economic, social, and political standpoint; and the critical subjects of Hijab, stoning, female mutilation, unequal inheritance, and polygamy.

The Spiritual Rights

According to the Quran, men and women have the same spirit. There is no superiority in the spiritual sense between men and women:

> O mankind! Be careful of your duty to your Lord
> Who created you from a single soul and from it
> created its mate and from them twain hath spread
> abroad a multitude of men and women. Be careful of
> your duty toward Allah in Whom ye claim (your
> rights) of one another, and toward the wombs, that
> bare you. Lo! Allah hath been a watcher over you.
> *(Quran 4:1)*

It is He who created you from one soul and created
from it its mate that he might dwell in security with
her... *(Quran 7:189)*

[He is] Creator of the heavens and the earth. He has
made for you from yourselves, mates... *(Quran 42:11)*

The Quran makes it clear that all human beings (and the
phraseology doesn't apply to men or women alone, but to both)
have what one might call a human spirit:

Breathed some of My spirit into divine touch. When
God created him [or her in this sense]. *(Quran 15:29.
See also 32:9)*

Some of His spirit here means not in the incarnational sense,
but the pure, innate spiritual nature that God has endowed her or
him with.

The Quran indicates again that one of the most honored
positions of humans is that God created the human, both sexes, as
His trustee and representative on earth. There are many references
in the Quran that confirm this.

Nowhere in the Quran is there any trace or any notion of
blaming Eve for the first mistake or for eating from the forbidden
tree. When the Quran speaks about Adam, Eve, and the forbidden
tree, it is in a totally different spirit. The story is narrated in 7:19 –
27, and it speaks about both of them doing this. Both of them
disobeyed. Both of them discovered the consequences of their
disobedience. Both of them sought repentance, and both of them
were forgiven.

Nowhere in the Quran does it say women are to be blamed for
the fall of man. Furthermore, when the Quran speaks about the

suffering of women during the period of pregnancy and childbirth, nowhere does it connect it with the original sin because there is no concept of original sin in Islam. All babies are born innocents. Suffering is presented as a reason to adore and love women. In the Quran, especially *31:14, 46:15*, it makes it quite clear God has commanded upon mankind to be kind to parents and mentions:

> His mother bore him in difficulty or suffering upon suffering. *(Quran 31:14, 46:15)*

The Quran makes it clear again to remove any notion of superiority for men, and I refer you again to *49:13*. I must caution that there are some mistaken translations, but in the original Arabic, there is no question of gender being involved.

In terms of moral and spiritual duties and acts of worship, the requirements of men and women are the same; however, in some cases women are given certain concessions because of their feminine nature, or their health, or the health of their babies. In these cases, it's a complete mercy and gift from God to women. For example, Muslim women don't pray the five obligatory prayers during menstruation or after delivering a baby. During these times, Muslim women don't fast and they are not required to do any kind of worship that requires effort. They are free from physical obligations; they just do their regular daily routine, relax, and remember God in some other way.

Also, Muslim men are required to attend Friday prayers at a mosque every week, but women can choose to attend or not. Either way, they are rewarded. This is one more special gift from God to Muslim women. I have to thank God that I don't have to leave my house or my job every Friday to go to the mosque.

More than one verse in the Quran, for example, 3:195 and 4:124, specify that whoever does good deeds, whether male or female, will receive an abundant reward from God.

The Prophet Muhammad also said, "Women are the twin halves of men." These were very direct clarifications from the Prophet about equality in Islam.

Economic Rights

We have to remember that in England until the 19th century, women did not have the right to own property. When she married, a woman's property would transfer to her husband, or she would not be able to dispense of it without his permission. In Britain, perhaps the first country to give women some property rights, laws were passed in the 1860s known as "Married Women Property Act." More than 1,300 years earlier, that right was clearly established in Islamic law:

> Men shall have the benefit of what they earn and
> women shall have the benefit of what they earn; and
> ask Allah of His grace; surely Allah knows all things.
> *(Quran 4:32)*

There is no restriction in Islamic law that says a Muslim woman can't work. In fact, in a truly Islamic society, there are women physicians, women nurses, and women teachers. If she chooses to work, she's entitled to equal pay. Muslim men are required to work and support the family, but Muslim women have the choice to work.

When it comes to financial security, Islamic law is more tilted in many respects towards women. These are some examples:

- During the period of engagement, a woman is to be on the receiving side of gifts.
- At the time of marriage, it is the duty of the husband, not the bride's family, to pay for a marital gift. The Quran called it a gift, and it is exclusively the right of the woman. She doesn't have to spend it on the household, and she doesn't have to give it to her father or anyone else.
- If a woman owns any property prior to marriage, she retains that property after marriage. It remains under her control. Also, in Muslim countries, a woman keeps her own last name and her own identity.
- If the woman has any earnings during her marriage, by way of investments of her property or as a result of work, she doesn't have to spend any money of that income on the household. It is exclusively hers.
- The full maintenance and support of a married woman is the entire responsibility of her husband even though she might be richer than he is. She doesn't have to spend a penny.
- At the time of a divorce, there are certain guarantees during the waiting period and even beyond for a woman's support.
- If the divorcee has children, she's entitled to child support.

The Social Rights

Education

The Prophet said "Learning is a duty on every Muslim," male and female. Muslim women were a very important part of leading sources of knowledge in early Islamic societies. Here I will give you an example. The University of al-Qarawiyyin is located in Fes, Morocco. It is the oldest existing, continually operating and the first degree-awarding educational institution in the world according to UNESCO (United Nation Educational, Scientific and Cultural Organization) and Guinness World Records, and is sometimes referred to as the oldest university. The Qarawiyyin, was founded by Fatima al-Fihri (a Muslim woman) in 859 and subsequently became one of the leading spiritual and educational centers of the world. The students of this university have studied theology, law, philosophy, mathematics, astronomy and languages. The university had among its students since the Middle Age famous people from all around the Mediterranean sea, such as the philosopher Averroes, the geographer Muhammad al-Idrisi and the important Jewish philosopher Maimonides. That was during the Golden Age of Islam, when Muslim women were very well educated and motivated to create the first organized place to spread knowledge around the world. During that time, thus Muslims were able to understand their religion and apply it to their lives. Unfortunately, the opposite is happening in the Muslim world today.

As a Daughter

We find that credit goes to Islam for stopping the barbaric practice of female infanticide in pre-Islamic Arabia. These ignorant people used to bury daughters alive. The Quran forbade the practice, making it a crime (in *Surah 81*). Additionally, the Quran condemned the chauvinistic attitudes of some people who used to greet the birth of a boy with gladness but the birth of a girl with sadness.

As far as treatment of daughters is concerned, Prophet Muhammad (peace be upon him) said, "Anyone who has two daughters, and did not insult them, but brought them up properly, he and I will be like this," holding his two fingers close together. Another version adds, "And also did not favor his sons over daughters." One time, the Prophet (peace be upon him) was sitting with a companion. The companion's son came, and he kissed his son and put him on his lap. Then his daughter came, and he just sat her by his side. The Prophet told the man, "You did not do justice," meaning he should have treated the daughter equally, kissed her and put her in his lap also. Indeed, whenever the Prophet's daughter Fatimah came to him in front of everyone, he stood up, kissed her, and let her sit in his favorite place where he'd been sitting.

As a Wife

From the marital standpoint, the Quran clearly indicates in *Surahs 30:20 and 42:11* that marriage is not just an inevitable evil. Marriage is not somebody getting married to his master or slave, but rather to his partner:

> Among His Signs is that he created for you mates
> from among yourselves, that they may dwell in
> tranquility with them, and He has put love and mercy
> between your (hearts): Verily in that are signs for
> those who reflect. *(Quran 30:21)*

166

There are numerous verses in the Quran to the same effect.

The approval and consent of the woman to marriage is a prerequisite for the validity of marriage in Islam. She has the right to say *yes* or *no*. The woman in Islam has the right to choose her husband. The marriage is not Islamic if she is not accepting her partner or was forced to marry him.

There is no arranged marriage in Islam, since the bride and the groom's acceptance are both required for an Islamic marriage.

Husbands' and wives' duties are mutual responsibilities. They might not be identical, but the totality of rights and responsibilities are balanced. The Quran says:

> And they (women) have rights (over their husbands)
> similar (to those of their husbands) over them, to
> what is reasonable, but men have a degree (of
> responsibility) over them. And Allah is All-Mighty,
> All-Wise. *(Quran 2:228)*

This only specifies the degree of responsibility, not privilege, in man's role as provider, protector, and maintainer of the family.

Muslim women are not required by the Shariah law to do all the house chores and errands. The husband is required to get the wife a maid if he financially can. And he is required to help her himself if he can't. Prophet Muhammad (peace be upon him) used to help in the house chores himself.

However, Muslim scholars have different opinions concerning the work of a woman in her house. The majority of Muslim scholars are of the opinion that serving one's husband is not compulsory, but consider it as a noble act of manners and kindness from the wife. Imams Maalik, Al Shafie, and Abu Haneefah, some of the most important and famous scholars in Islamic history, supported this opinion. Imam Ibn El Qayyim cited that an Islamic marriage contract enables a husband to enjoy his wife; it doesn't engage her in housework.

Also, Muslims' wives are not required to serve their in-laws. If some Muslim men force their wives to do so, it's cultural behavior, and it has absolutely no connection with the religion of Islam. If wives choose to do so, they are rewarded from God, but they don't have to.

As a Mother
The Quran placed obedience to and caring for parents immediately after worship of God.

> We have enjoined mankind to be kind and care for
> his/her parents. *(Quran 31:14)*

Islam speaks of mothers in a very succinct statement. Once a man came to Prophet Muhammad (peace be upon him) and asked, "O, Messenger, who among mankind is worthy of my kindness and love?" The Prophet answered, "Your mother." "Who next?" "Your mother." "Who next?" "Your mother." Only after the third time he said, "And your father."

We find the Quran says men and women they should cooperate and collaborate in goodness. *Surah 9:71* speaks about men and women as supporters and helpers of each other, ordaining the good and forbidding the evil, establishing prayers, and giving charity. Prophet Muhammad (peace be upon him) echoed what the Quran said. "I command you to be kind to women." In one of his last commands during his farewell pilgrimage before his death, he kept repeating, "I command you to be kind and considerate to women." In another hadith (saying), he said, "It is only the generous in character who is good to women, and only the evil one who insults them."

Divorce

The Quran talks about consultation between husband and wife even in the case of divorce. When there are family disputes, the Quran first appeals to reason and the consideration of positive aspects of one's spouse:

> Dwell with your wives in kindness, for even if you
> hate them, you might be hating someone in whom
> God has placed so much good. *(Quran 4:19)*

If a divorce becomes necessary, there are many detailed procedures in Islamic law that really knock down the common notion that divorce in Islam is very easy and that it is the sole right of man. It is not the sole right of man, nor is it true that all he has to do is say three times, *I divorce you,* and that's it. Islam also has laws regarding custody of children. I was very surprised to see newspapers making the false claim that, in all cases, custody goes to the father. Custody involves the interest of the child, and laws often favor the mother of young children.

In Islam, a woman also has the right to ask for a separation from her husband if she is not happy or is afraid of being harmed by him. Also, she can request under an Islamic marriage contract to have the right to take the decision of divorcing.

Inheritance

Here we can talk about why the Islamic laws pertaining to inheritance give men in some cases a higher share. All of a man's inheritance is most likely for related women, such as his mother, wife, sister, or daughter, because men are the providers in Islam.

On the other hand, all of a woman's inheritance is most likely for herself, according to the religion's rules. Also, we have to know that, in the Shariah, there are cases when a male inherits twice the share of a female; in other cases, they have equal shares, and, still in a few cases, a female can inherit a larger share than a male.

Political Rights

In the most authentic collection of hadith, Hadith Bukhari, a section is devoted to the participation of women, not only in public affairs but also in the battlefield and as logistical support. Muslim men are required to protect the society and create an army. Muslim women always have had their own choice to join or not. In Islamic history, Muslim women carried arms, and when there was great danger to the Muslims, they volunteered to participate in the battlefield. Also, Prophet Muhammad (peace and prayers be upon him) asked the women to vote and for their agreement to the first Islamic constitution, when he started establishing the Islamic state in Madina more than 1,400 years ago.

Hijab

Hijab is used to cover a woman's hair and the body. Hijab is a sign of modesty and chastity in Islam, and it is related to high moral values. Hijab is not just for women; men are also required to wear a certain type of Hijab, to cover the body from the navel to the knees. Covering the head with a small white cap or an Islamic turban is what the Prophet used to do. In my opinion, the difference just clarifies the importance and the great value of a woman's body.

Hijab as covering for women was mentioned and practiced in religions and cultures prior to Islam. In Christianity, it is mentioned in *1 Corinthians 11:5*. Because of that, I saw many Christian women in Egypt would cover their hair with a scarf before they went for a prayer in church. Also, I've seen many Jewish orthodox women wearing exactly what any Muslim women would wear as Hijab. Modesty is still an important value in our world, not just from a religious perspective, but also as a sign of respect and dignity. I don't think that I would ever see the Queen of England or any of the princesses any time, anywhere in a micro-skirt or a very open dress.

In Islam, a woman's body is not for anyone to enjoy except the one who deserves it, and who makes strong commitments to protect it and values it in a legal marriage.

Almost 99.9% of Muslim Hijabi women I have met in my life in Egypt, Saudi Arabia, or the U.S. chose to wear Hijab as a kind of worship and remembrance of God. No one forced them to wear it. But what about the Muslim women shown in the Western media? Were they forced to cover their faces?

Niqab, or the covering of body and face is another kind of worshiping. In the majority of the Islamic scholars' opinions, niqab is not required in the religion of Islam. All the woman whom I have met in my life that wear niqab actually chose to wear it. And in most cases, their families disapproved of their decision to wear niqab.

One of my non-Muslim friends sent me an article about how Muslim women are suffering because they are being forced to cover in Muslim countries. To understand this point, I need to share some facts. The only two countries that force their women to cover are Saudi Arabia and Iran. These are two of 49 Muslim-majority countries in the world. The Muslim populations of these two countries is 28 million and 77 million, respectively, which totals 105 million people. If we consider half of this number to be women, then it's around 53 million women in both countries, out of 800 million Muslim women worldwide. This means that 6% of all Muslim women are forced to wear Hijab or to be covered. That is only if we consider all the women in these two countries are *forced*, which is not true. (In some Saudi Arabian cities women don't have to cover their faces.) If half of them are forced, then only 3% of the Muslim women in the world are forced to cover. But the media in the West focuses so much on this small percentage and forgets all the rest of the Hijabi Muslim women like myself who, with all their free will, choose to wear Hijab. (I refer you to the first chapter– My Hijab on Page 19.)

Female Mutilation

This is a problem, but mostly an African problem, not an Islamic problem. This act is very common in many Christian countries in Africa, such as Eritrea, Ethiopia, and others, and a couple of Islamic African countries, such as Egypt and Sudan. However, it's not common to find this act in most other Islamic countries on different continents. This act is very common in some Islamic countries among illiterate families. Because male mutilation exists in Islam as in Judaism, they think female mutilation is as important, so it's most likely practiced for cultural reasons.

Stoning

There are some verses in the Torah that mention stoning.

> And all the men of his city shall stone him with
> stones, so that he die. So shalt thou put evil away

from among you, and all Israel shall hear and fear.
(Deuteronomy 21:21)

You can find it in other verses of the Old Testament, such as
1 Kings 21:10 and *Leviticus 24:10–16*. Stoning was a very common
act in many other religions and cultures before Islam.

The word stoning is never mentioned in the Quran, which is
the first source of the Shariah law. The only punishment for
adultery that is mentioned in the Quran is lashing. Stoning was
done once during Prophet Muhammad's (peace and prayers be
upon him) life (at the request of the sinner herself), and that's why
some people see this as approval for stoning. But I totally agree
with the opinion of the great Islamic scholar Dr. Mostafa Mahmoud
on this point. He said that, most likely, the Prophet did that before
the revelation of Surah Al Nour (The Chapter of Light) which
came with the new Islamic law for adultery. He brought great
proofs from the Quran and sunnah for his opinion.

Any Islamic scholar who agrees with stoning believes in these
points:

- The society has to be Islamic and all Muslims agree on
  practicing all the Islamic retributions.
- The punishment for adultery for an unmarried
  individual is lashing and for a married individual is
  stoning.
- A stoning is for a married person who has committed
  adultery with someone other than his or her marriage
  partner in such a way that four witnesses saw
  everything.
- The four adult witnesses have to be known for their
  honesty and have to see the moment of adultery

(intercourse). If one of them is not honest enough, that will cancel the retribution.

○ If three honest witnesses (or fewer than four) saw that and mentioned names of the sinners, these three people will be lashed the same number of lashes or suffer stoning rather than the ones who committed the sin.

○ If the person who committed adultery is Muslim, who knows very well about the punishment for what he/she committed, he/she will be stoned. If the person is not a Muslim, a traveler, or new to the community, the fact that he/she didn't know the consequences of his/her actions will be enough to cancel the retribution.

As you see, for all these points to occur, stoning or lashing is rare possibility.

I remember a beautiful story about Umar ibn Al Khatab, who was one of the closest companions to Prophet Muhammad (peace be upon him). He was the second Caliph and was known for his honesty and fairness. One day, he was walking on the streets at night and saw two people he knew having sex in a field. He went the next day to the Muslim judge who was Ali ibn Abu Talib, the Prophet's cousin, the fourth Caliph, and another of the best companions. Umar told Ali about what he had seen in the field, so Ali asked, "Did three honest people see that with you?" Umar said, "No! But you know I never lie." Ali said, "If you mention these two sinners' names, you are the one who will be lashed; it's not my rules, it's God's rules." Notice the Muslim judge was actually talking to the Caliph, the most important person in that society back then, and he was sure Umar was not lying. That's how

Shariah was very firm in protecting the privacy and the reputation of the human, man or woman, sinner or not.

Here is another important point to share; the punishment, lashing or stoning, is it just for women?

Shariah is very clear about any criminal's or sinner's punishment: men and women are exactly the same in every single detail.

Polygamy

It has become mythical in the minds of many people that being Muslim means having four wives. This is a false notion, of course. A very renowned anthropologist, Edward Westermarck, in his two-volume work, *History of Human Marriage*, notes that there has been polygamy in virtually every culture and religion, including Judaism and Christianity. But the point here is not to say, "Why blame Islam?" Actually, even among Abrahamic faiths Islam, in its holy book, is the only religion that specifically limited the practice of polygamy existing before Islam, and established some very strict conditions for guidance.

The question, "How could any man have two wives? That's terrible!" reflects ethnocentrism. We assume that, because we're living in the West and it seems strange, monogamy should apply to all cultures, at all times, and under all circumstances. This simply isn't true. Until now, in the American west, some Mormon groups practice polygamy as a part of their religion.

Polygamy is not really accepted in my Egyptian culture, but during my early life in Saudi Arabia, I was surprised that having more than one wife is very normal. The first wife accepted that to the point that she was the one who picked her husband's second wife for him. Also, she was the one who planned the wedding for them!

As I see here in the West the man is only allowed to have one wife, but is she always *the only* woman in his life?

But why would God allow the men ever to marry more than one? As we believe, Islam is the end of God's messages to earth and it should be able to solve any problem any time with the least losses. Let me give an example: during wars many lose their lives, a great majority of whom are usually men of a marriageable age. Now, with a great shortage of men, what will happen to their widows, their orphans, and their daughters of marriageable age? Is it better to leave them in a camp with a handout? Or is it better when a man is willing to take care of this widow and her children?

The only verse in the whole Quran that speaks about polygamy speaks about limiting, not instituting, polygamy. The verse was revealed right after the Battle of Uhud, in which many Muslims were martyred for the first time and left behind many wives and children in need of support. This verse shows the spirit and reason of the revelation. It was a way to protect as many women as possible and not to humiliate them.

Also, according to many Islamic scholars, many preconditions have to be met before thinking about polygamy; for example, wars, sickness, and the acceptance of the first wife who can ask for divorce. The man has to be physically and financially capable to marry more than one. He has to deal with his wives fairly, or he is not allowed to marry more than one. Also, the wife has the right in Islam to make her marriage contract conditional, so that her husband will not be allowed to have a second wife.

I have heard some stories, as you might have, about husbands who cheat on their wives with other women for years; these stories are proof to me that having one wife is not always the case in the West either. I see cheating as a form of polygamy, but with no protection for the main families or the other women.

Now I hope it is clearer to you that the problems present in some societies are not the problems of Islam itself, but problems of a lack of commitment, lack of application, or misapplication of Islamic teachings by Muslims themselves. The topics I have tried to cover here represent the big gap that exists between the true teachings of Islam as derived from its original sources and its projected image in the West, as well as the way some Muslims disregard those noble teachings. One of the most expressive sentences I heard about this is "Islam is perfect, but Muslims are not. Judge me by my actions, but don't judge my religion by my actions."

Sources

- *Being a Muslim* by Haroon Siddiqui
- *Clear Your Doubts About Islam; 50 Answers to common Questions*, Saheeh International, editor
- *Women Rights in Islam* by Dr. Zakir Naik
- Dr. Mostafa Mahmoud articles
- http://www.islamswomen.com/
- http://www.islamweb.net/

20   U.S. and Me

To explain and discuss a very critical subject like the one I chose for this chapter is not easy at all, but I promise to be honest in every single word because this time it's not just me, but billions of people with me.

First I need to tell you some very important information about Muslims and Arabs:

  - ○ Muslims and Arabs are two different things. Muslims all around the world are 1.6 billion. The majority of them are NOT Arab; just 15% of them are Arab. And to be honest, they are not the best Muslims because of their societies.

  - ○ Muslims are spread all over the world. They speak the language of their home countries, and some non-Arab Muslims learn Arabic to recite the Qur'an in its original revelation language.

  - ○ The largest populations of Muslims are in Indonesia, then the Indian subcontinent; large numbers of Muslims speak, as a daily language, Bahasa Indonesia, Urdu, Bengali, and English, in addition to those in the Arab world who speak Arabic. So now when I talk about myself or my country you will have a clearer picture in your mind.

I Hate Politics

I spent the first ten years of my life in Egypt and the Kingdom of Saudi Arabia (KSA); during that time, I didn't hear or know anything about U.S. except just one thing, the soap opera "Knots Landing." Thus, in my mind, the U.S. was all nice houses and beautiful people.

In the second ten years, my image of the U.S. was totally different. I started to watch more TV and news. I heard more about politics. I learned about Hiroshima. I saw that so many Muslims and Christians are killed by Israel's army every day in Palestine. Every time the United Nations wanted to make a law to stop that with the majority of countries, the U.S. would come out with a veto; so the United Nations couldn't do it! Then I knew that the U.S. is the country that giving the most support to Israel by sending them all kinds of weapon, with billions of dollars every year. And I saw the Israelis using it to take more land from the Palestinians and kill more of them. I always asked myself why?

Every time I saw on Egyptian TV the awful images of those children and people who were killed in cold blood, I just imagined myself as one of them. Between Palestine and Egypt there are only a few kilometers. I thought everything that was happening to those people in Palestine could happen to me one day with the support of the U.S. That was not a farfetched possibility, since Israel had occupied a part of Egypt, but the Egyptian army was able to get it back in 1973 before I was born.

I remember most of my friends dreamed about living abroad either in Europe or U.S. since they knew they would have much better opportunities for easier life, but I never had this dream. Maybe that was because I spent most of my childhood outside

Egypt, or because I had so many dreams for Egypt in my mind and wanted to be part of achieving them one day.

Unexpected Changes

The idea of me living outside my city was totally rejected by my family and me, and up to this moment that I'm writing, I still don't know how my husband was able to convince me and the whole family to take this step in a very short time. It seemed like the next moment I was in the TWA plane, watching the sky from the window with a combination of feelings, mostly nervous. I couldn't even picture my life in the U.S. The main thing in my heart was created from the American movies and politics, that *I will not be welcome* even though I was not wearing Hijab back then; I was still uncomfortable.

I still remember that moment when the plane started to land, and I began to see more features of the American land, with a beautiful design of landscaping and new life for me!

However, my first two years were the worst ever. I was away from my family and friends, unable to speak English well and fearing to even try. I couldn't understand TV. It cost me $3.00 per minute to call my family in Egypt. You can just imagine how hard it was!

The only thing I noticed during that time was how bad the media talked about Muslims, both directly and indirectly. Also, it always bothered me how they showed any Arab or Muslim character in the American movies as either evil or stupid.

Then, the 9/11 disaster happened. I remember that moment very well. When my husband came home early from work and I was sleeping, he woke me up and said, "Get up and watch the TV. See what is happening in the world."

U.S. and Me

We ran to the living room and turned the TV on, and I heard them saying they suspected that some Muslims did it. I screamed to my husband's face, "Why do they keep accusing Muslims all the time? They don't know how killing is forbidden in Islam? How come they knew after five minutes who did it? It is too fast to say it before any investigations." I was so mad and sure that they were just lying on the TV. IT IS IMPOSSIBLE! NO PRACTICING MUSLIM WOULD EVER THINK TO DO THAT!

You all know the rest of this story, and I have heard so many scenarios for it and can't really tell which one made more sense to me.

All the Muslims, including my kids and I are paying for 9/11 every day. I remember when my son was in third grade; he came back from school on 9/11 and told me, "Mom, my friend is lying to me. Our teacher was talking about the attacks and he whispered to me, *These people were Muslims like you*. Mommy, he was lying, right? You told me it is forbidden to hurt or kill anyone in Islam."

I started to explain to him that in every religion there are good and bad people, and that never comes from the religion but from the people themselves. Inside me, I was sad that he heard that at such a young age.

Despite all the changes around me, I was preparing myself for an internal change. It was a challenge when I decided to wear my Hijab after 9/11. My husband kept pushing me and encouraging me to go out, meet people and talk with them. Finally, I listened to him. My first time going out by myself was a ladies' bingo game at my complex clubhouse that took place every Wednesday.

It was a full shock for me. These people were so nice; they welcomed me. They didn't mind my bad English with my awful accent; they smiled at me all the time, and even one of them mentioned that she liked my scarf! Oh my goodness! I could not believe it!

The Clear Picture

One of the movies that had the greatest effect on my feelings was *How to Train Your Dragon*. The idea was that some people saw dragons as very dangerous, evil, and scary creatures. These people's mission in life was to kill the dragons to save earth. The mission changed when a little boy couldn't see himself as a killer and wanted to treat the dragons in a different way. He wanted to discover their lives. Then, a miracle happened! He found out that they were trying to kill people just to defend themselves and not to destroy them. He started to communicate with the dragons; they helped him and he saved them. I think this movie may explain a lot!

How To Train Your Dragon may show the two halves of the world. The only difference is that they are both humans, but they are seeing each other as dangerous dragons. If both give themselves the opportunity to show the real human part in each other, surely the world would be a much better place. Muslims and Arabs are not all terrorists and Americans are not all evil.

I was sitting with my parents watching a soccer game between Egypt and another team a long time ago. We all cheered for Egypt. The next game was between Kingdom of Saudi Arabia and another team. I found out that my parents were cheering for the Saudi Arabian team. I stopped, looked at them and asked my mom, "Mom, why are you both cheering for the KSA team when it's not our country?" She said, "Rania, we ate from their land. We had so many fun days with their people, and we worked hard for their schools and companies for years. I think that it is only right to cheer for them." Do you remember these kinds of words in your childhood? The words that might build something in your mind, soul, and personality. These words were just like that for me!

I have all these feelings for the U.S. This country is not politics or governments. It is the awesome people I met, the kind hearts I found, and the warm and nice friends I made. It is the place that gave me a great opportunity to learn and grow. It is the land I had my boys in. The land I knew and studied my religion in, like I never did before. It is a place where I felt the freedom to practice my religion, visit the mosque, and wear my Hijab. It is a variety of people—all colors, races, cultures, and beliefs—whom I met and learned from.

If you ask me, *would I have ever thought I might have all those feeling for the U.S.*, my answer would be NO! I never thought I would have an American friend and would love her like my own blood sister. When she experiences pain, I cry with her, and when she is happy, my heart is filled with joy. This is the humanity that we all have, and which I discovered when I came here.

In March 2008, I went to the courthouse to say the pledge of allegiance, the anthem and receive my citizenship certificate to be an American citizen. With many other people from many different countries around the world, we all repeated the pledge and the anthem. Then, the judge said, "Now all of you are Americans, just like me and any other American out there. Never feel that you are less a citizen than anyone who was born in this country. You have the same exact rights and have the same exact duties. The only thing that you will not be able to do as any other American after you go out of this room, is to be the president of the United

States." His golden words are always in my heart, and it helps me anytime I face any challenge during my life in the U.S.

As a Muslim woman, I have faced challenges from some people. But there are more good people, and they deserve to be mentioned more than anything else. Without everything that happened to me here, and without everyone I met here and without everything I learned here, I would never have become who I am now. Because of that, my mission in my Arabic writings is to show the Arab people who never got the chance to visit the U.S. the real beauty and tolerance in the Americans whom I have met here. And my mission in my English writing is to show Americans, who don't know about Islam except from the media, the real and true beauty of my religion and my culture. I will keep doing that until the end of my life, to help make a better and more understanding world for my life and my children's lives.

Respect!

Afterword
by Evemarie Moore

I hope you liked *America Through My Eyes* as much as I did. When a copy of it was handed to me recently by a mutual friend, so that I could check it for anything not agreeing with orthodox Islam (but please note: orthodox, not fundamentalist), I had no idea who the author was. But while reading her creation, I found her smart, and knowledgeable, warm-hearted, and insightful. I started to feel that she was not just a person I would like to meet, but whom I already knew, who was my friend; and instead of looking for mistaken opinions on Islam (yes, I did that, too, although without success), instead I found myself in conversation with her, and wrote all over her copy, notes like, *Yes, that happened to me, too*, or *Yes, my mother always liked to visit me in the U.S. because Americans are so friendly*. You can see what I mean.

If you come to know something about Islam, you will find there are many Islams: that of the Sufi, that of the Legal Scholar, that of the man or woman in the street; and they can all be legitimate Muslims. Those who hate you and want to do you in, they may think they are Muslims, but we—you, and I, and Rania—know they are not. This is not the model our Prophet set. And having read Rania's book, you know that now, too.

Evemarie Moore is a German convert to Islam as well as a retired technical writer; she studied at Chicago Islamic College and now lives in Chicago.

Acknowledgments

Many thanks and appreciation to

- Glen Heefner for his outstanding support and help in making my dream book a reality.

- The writers group of the Plano Illinois community library for their help editing my writings and giving me courage to think of this dream and believe I can achieve it. The amazing writers are David Dean, Jeanne Valentine, Vivian Wright, Paul Block, Becca Morello, Kristy Gravlin, John Dixon, Rosemary Walter, Kent Svendsen, and Anne Marie Claahsen.

- My special American friends who always are ready to help me and my English any day at any time: Jodi Sell and Shalley Wakeman.

- My English teachers in Egypt, especially my dad. Those who helped me to learn English and English writing in the U.S., especially Angela Krischon and my English Professors Lise Schlosser and Randall Earley.

- My husband Mohamed Aly for creating the cover design and for everything else he did to help me achieve my dream.

- My book's graphic designer Huda Muhammad Abdelgawad.

Acknowledgments

- Sarah Hussain for editing some of my chapters.

- Evemarie Moore for her great help in this book.

- All my true friends who give my life the best meaning with their love and support.

- YOU for taking the time to read my words.

Made in the USA
Middletown, DE
24 August 2019